The Complete Book of
Numbers & Counting

Thinking Kids™
Carson-Dellosa Publishing LLC
Greensboro, North Carolina

1 2 3 4 5 9 6 7 10 8

1 2 3 4 5 6 7 8 9 10 11

8 8 9 2 3 4

Thinking Kids™
Carson-Dellosa Publishing LLC
P.O. Box 35665
Greensboro, NC 27425 USA

Printed in the USA • All rights reserved.
01-032161151

ISBN 978-1-4838-2690-5

Table of Contents

Number Recognition

Number 0

Color the number. **Color** the word.

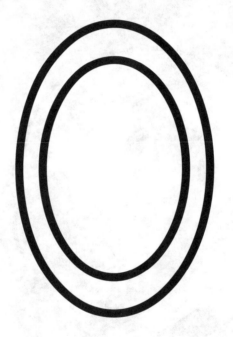

zero

Name _____

Number 0

 **Trace** the number.

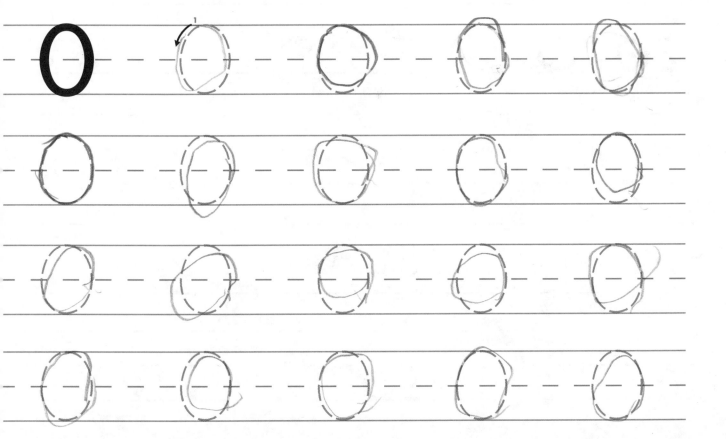

Name_____

Zero

 **Trace** the word.

zero

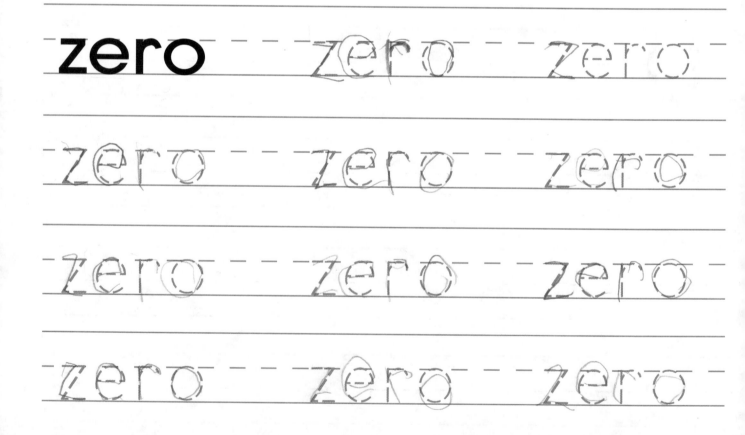

zero   zero   zero

zero   zero   zero

zero   zero   zero

zero   zero   zero

Name_____

Write 0

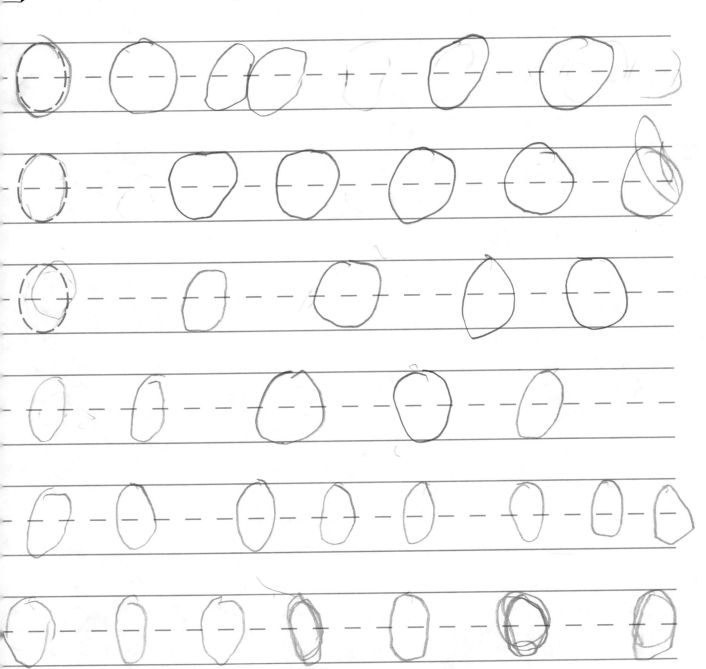

Now practice **writing** the number by yourself on the lines below.

Name_____

Write Zero

Now practice **writing** the word by yourself on the lines below.

zero

zero

zero

Name_____

Number 1

Color the number. **Color** the word. **Color** the rest of the picture.

Trace 1

Trace the number.

I

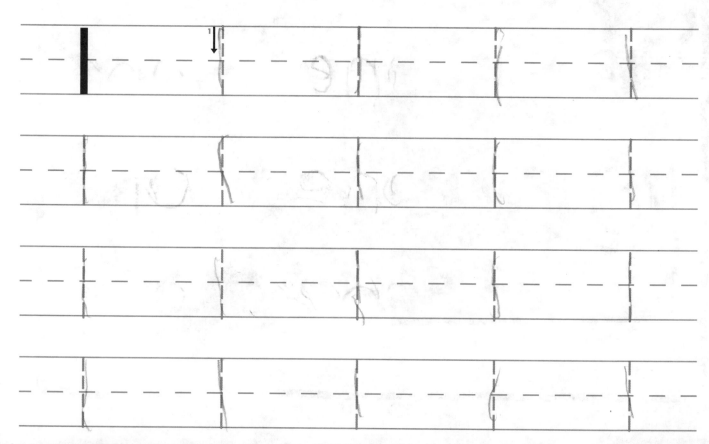

Name_____

Trace One

 Trace the word.

one

one   one   one

one   one   one

one   one   one

one   one   one

Write I

Now practice **writing** the number by yourself on the lines below.

Name_____

Write One

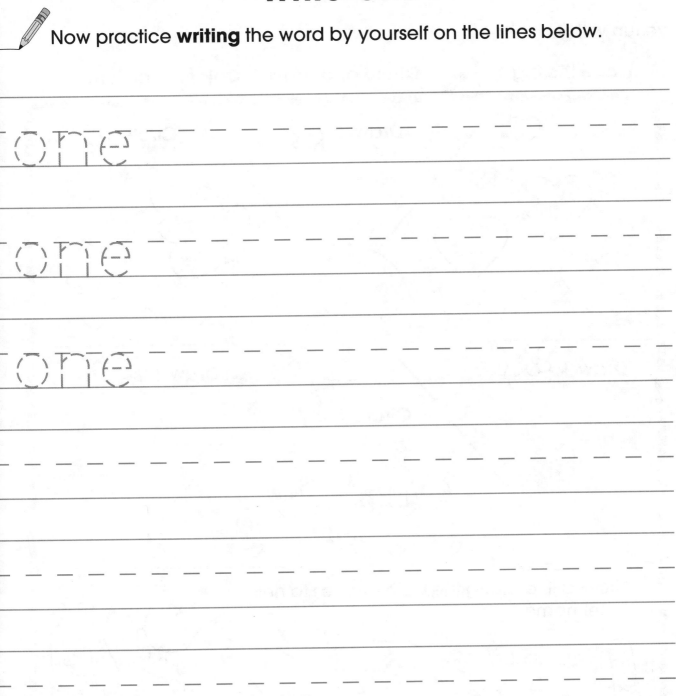

Now practice **writing** the word by yourself on the lines below.

Name_____

Have Fun with 1

Have fun with **1**!

Trace the big **1**. **Circle** and **draw** **1**. **Color** the pictures.

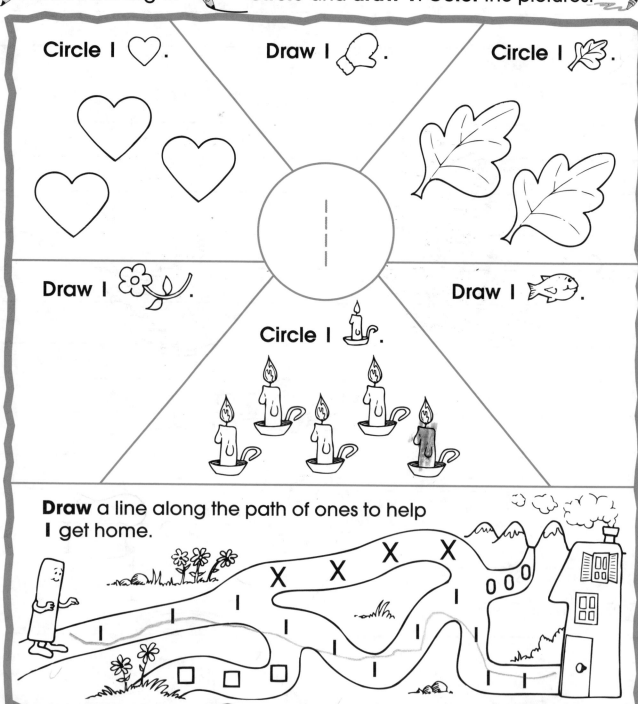

Circle 1 ♡.

Draw 1 🧤.

Circle 1 🍂.

Draw 1 🌼.

Draw 1 🐟.

Circle 1 🕯.

Draw a line along the path of ones to help **1** get home.

Name_____

Count and Color 1

ount and **color.**

Trace each **1**. **Color 1** red ___ , **1** blue ___ , and

green. ___

Name _____

One of a Kind

 Color the spaces: **l** - **green**   ● - **brown**   **one** - **blue**

What is it?

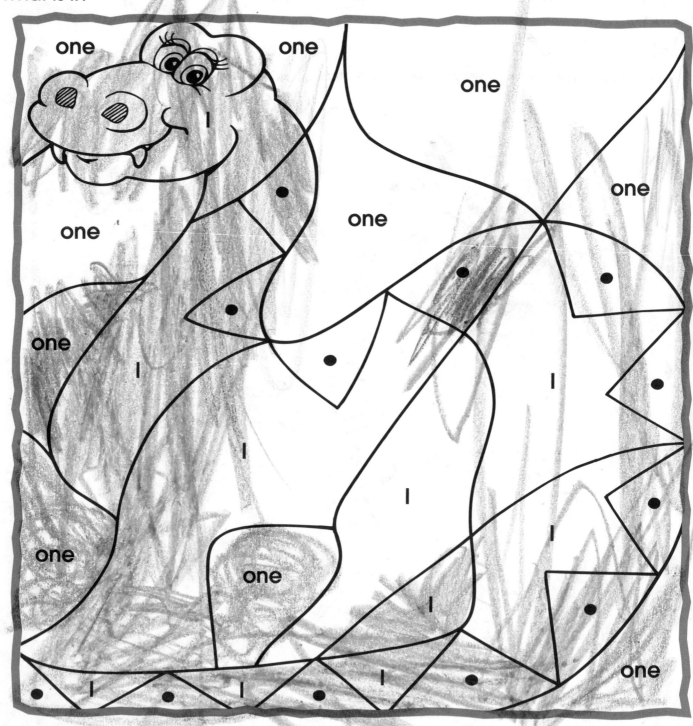

Name _____

Number 2

Color the number. **Color** the word. **Color** the rest of the picture.

Trace 2

✏ **Trace** the number.

2

Name_____

Trace Two

✏️ **Trace** the word.

two

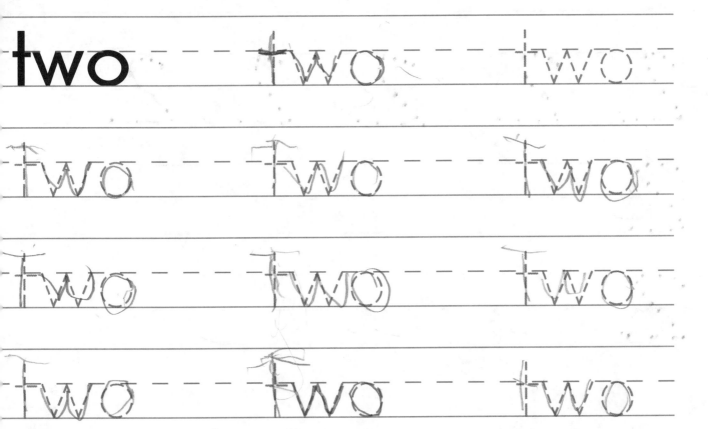

two   two   two

two   two   two

two   two   two

two   two   two

Name_____

Write 2

Now practice **writing** the number by yourself on the lines below.

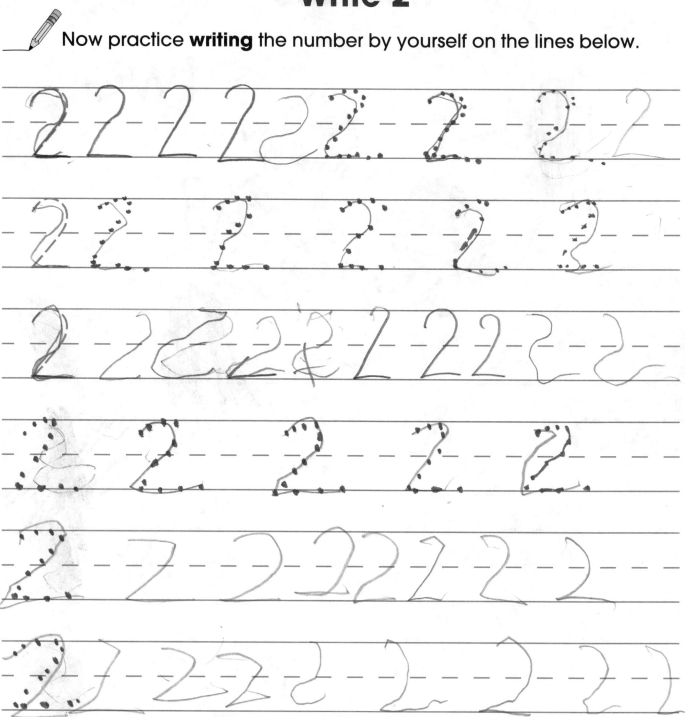

Name_____

Write Two

Now practice **writing** the word by yourself on the lines below.

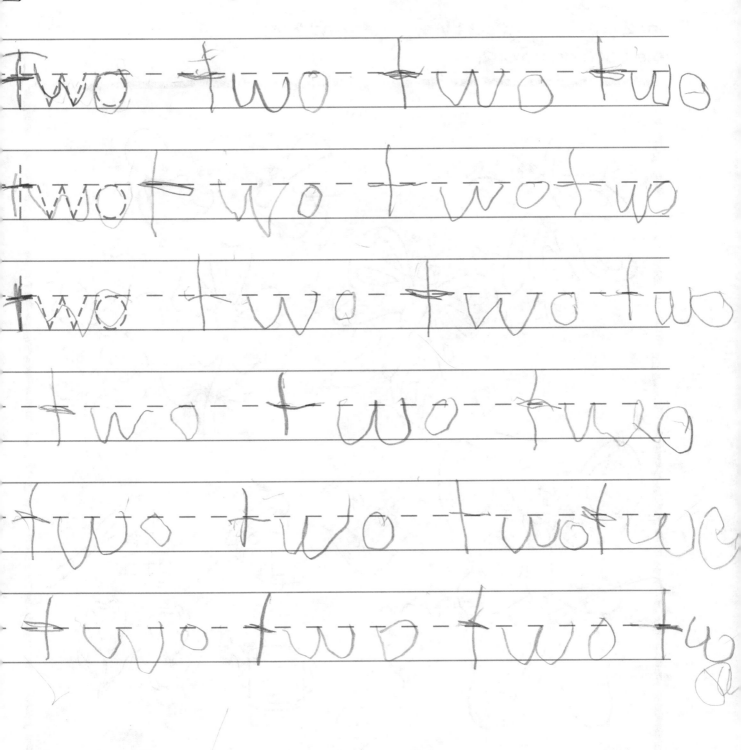

Name_____

Count and Color 2

Count and **color** each picture.

Color 2 yellow, **2 blue**, and **2 red**.
Circle each group of **2**.

Name_____

More to Do with 2

Trace each **2**. **Color** the flowers: **2 red,** **2 purple,** and **2 yellow.** **Circle** each with a **2**.

Name_____

Very Cool 2

Color the spaces: **2 - black**   **two - blue**   **I - white**   ● ● - orange

What is it?

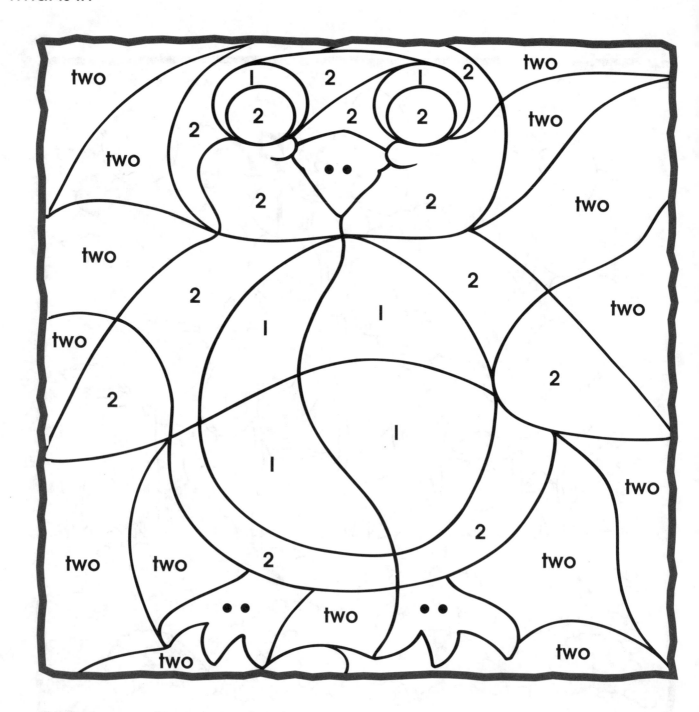

Name_____

Number 3

Color the number. **Color** the word. **Color** the rest of the picture.

Name_____

Trace 3

 Trace the number.

3

Name

Trace Three

Trace the word.

three

three three three

three three three

three three three

three three three

Name_____

Write 3

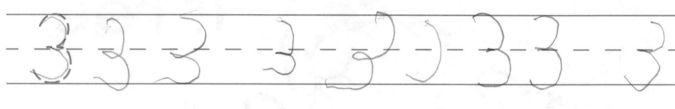

Now practice **writing** the number by yourself on the lines below.

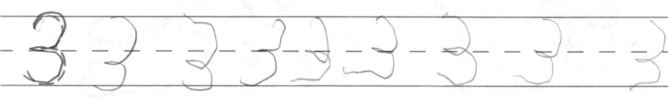

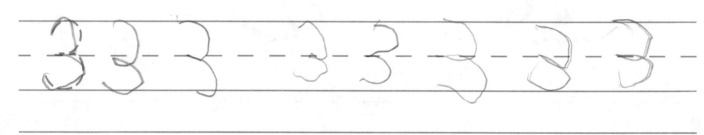

Name_____

Write Three

Now practice **writing** the word by yourself on the lines below.

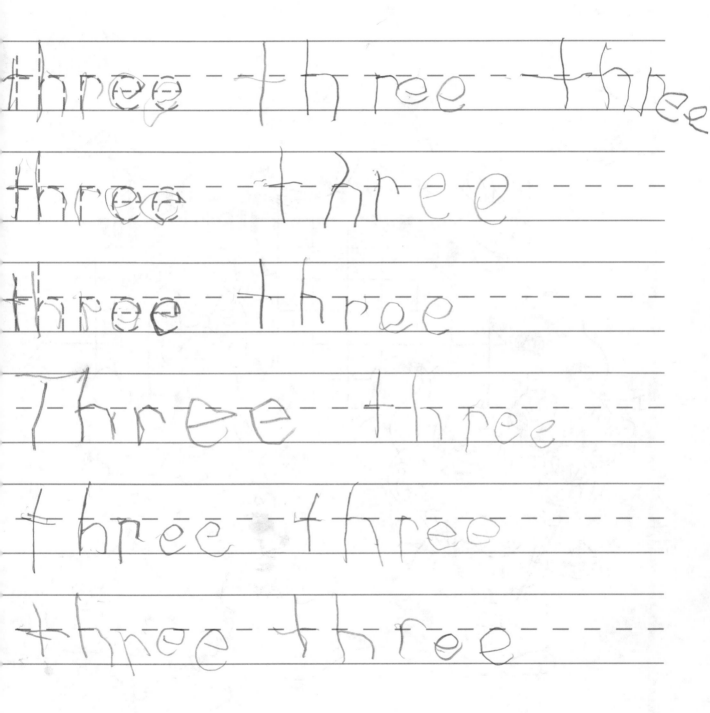

Name_____

Circle 3

Circle each group of **3**. **Color** the whole picture.

Name_____

Draw 3

Draw 3 s in the pen. **Color** the pigs.

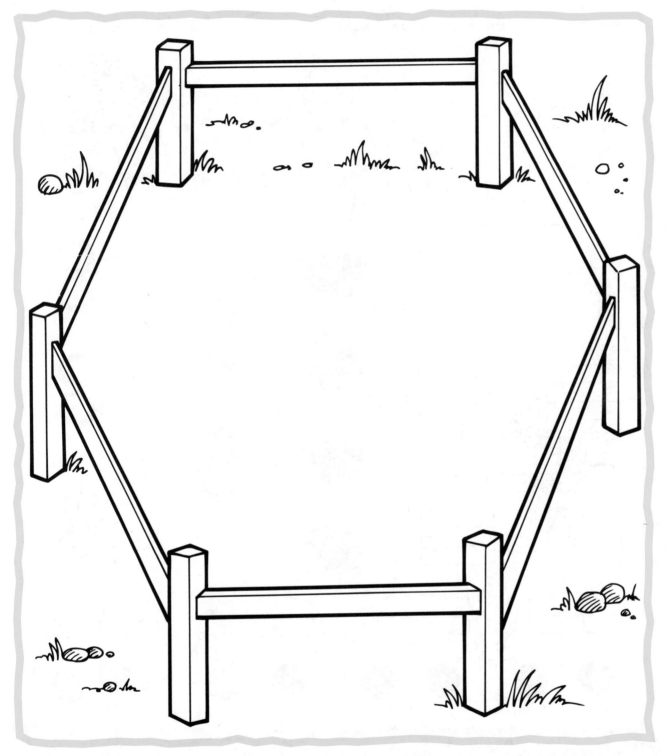

Name_____

Circle 3

Circle 3 things in each group. Color the pictures that are circled.

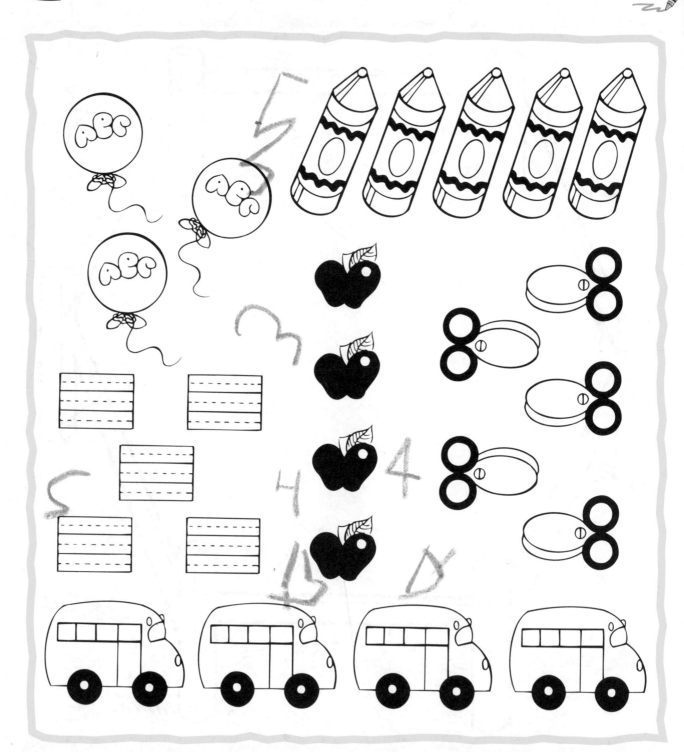

Name_____

Number 4

Color the number. **Color** the word. **Color** the rest of the picture.

Trace 4

Trace the number.

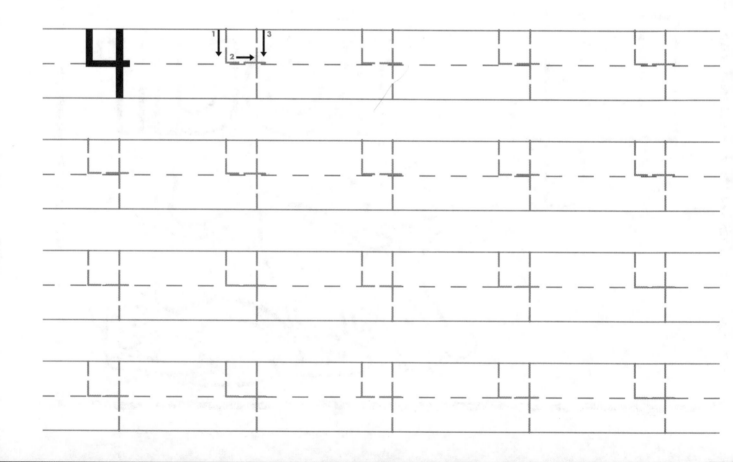

Name _____

Trace Four

Trace the word.

four

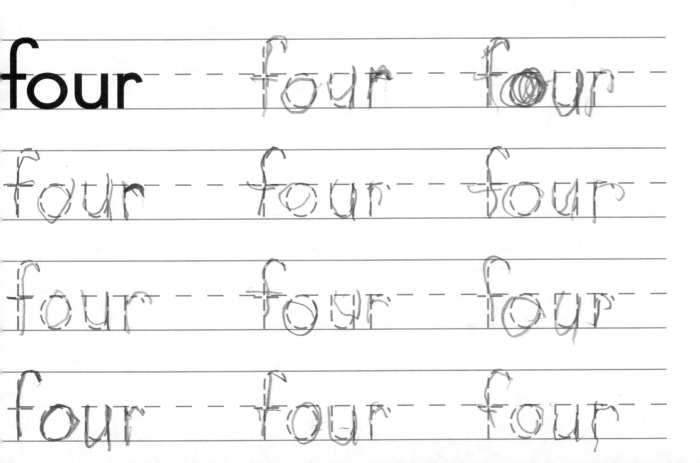

four   four   four

four   four   four

four   four   four

four   four   four

Name_____

Write 4

Now practice **writing** the number by yourself on the lines below.

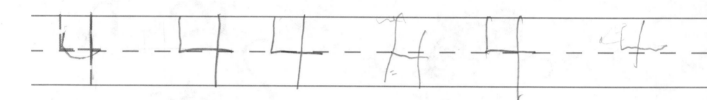

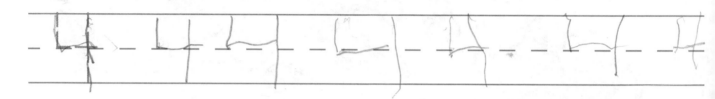

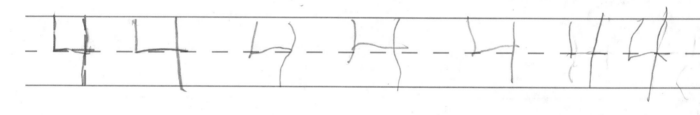

Name_____

Write Four

Now practice **writing** the word by yourself on the lines below.

four

four

four

four

four

Name_____

Circle 4 Things

Circle 4 things in each group.   **Trace** each **4**.

Color the picture.

Name_____

Where are the 4's?

Where are the **4's**?

Circle the **4's**. **Color** the picture.

Name_____

Very Cool 4

 Color the spaces: **4** - *yellow*   •• - *orange*   **four** - **blue**   **3** - **black**

What is it?

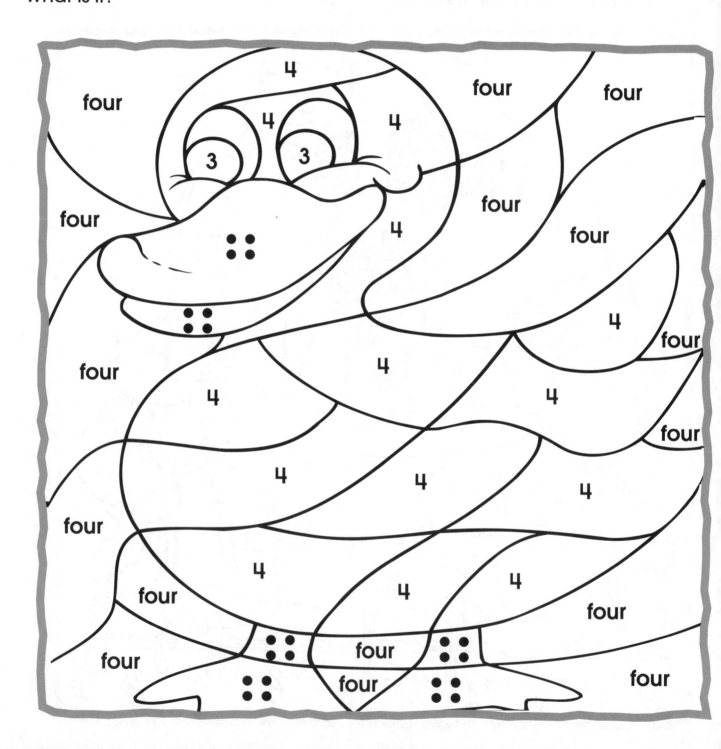

Name_____

Number 5

Color the number. **Color** the word. **Color** the rest of the picture.

Name_____

Trace 5

✏️ **Trace** the number.

Name_____

Trace Five

✏️ **Trace** the word.

five

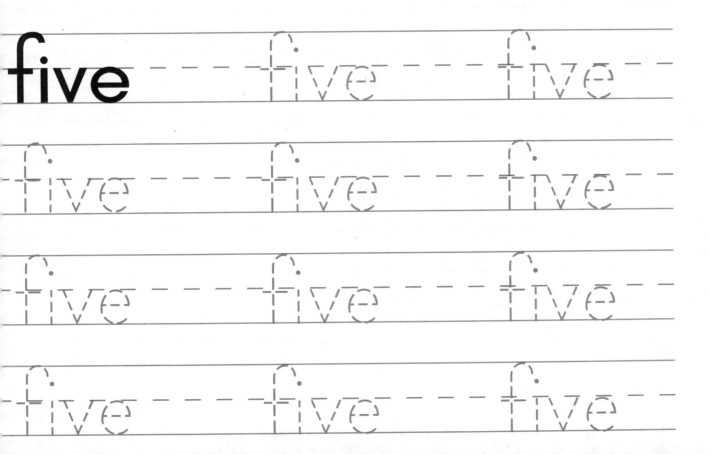

Name_____

Write 5

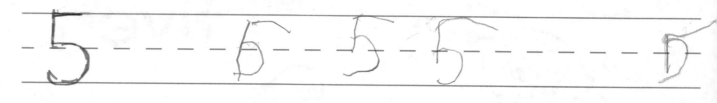 Now practice **writing** the number by yourself on the lines below.

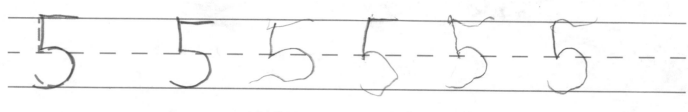

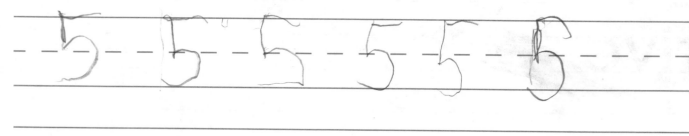

Name_____

Write Five

Now practice **writing** the word by yourself on the lines below.

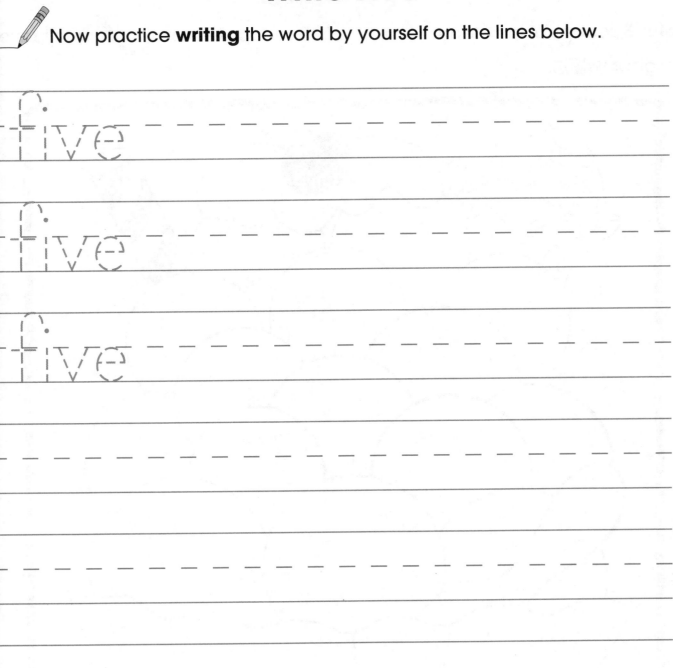

Name_____

Color 5

Color 5 scoops of ice cream **pink**,  **5** scoops **brown**, and leave **5** scoops **white**.

Name_____

Draw 5

Draw an **X** on each group of **5** dolphins diving through a hoop!

Name_____

Count and Color 5

Count and **color** each picture.   **Trace** the dotted line from **1–5**.

Circle each group of **5**.

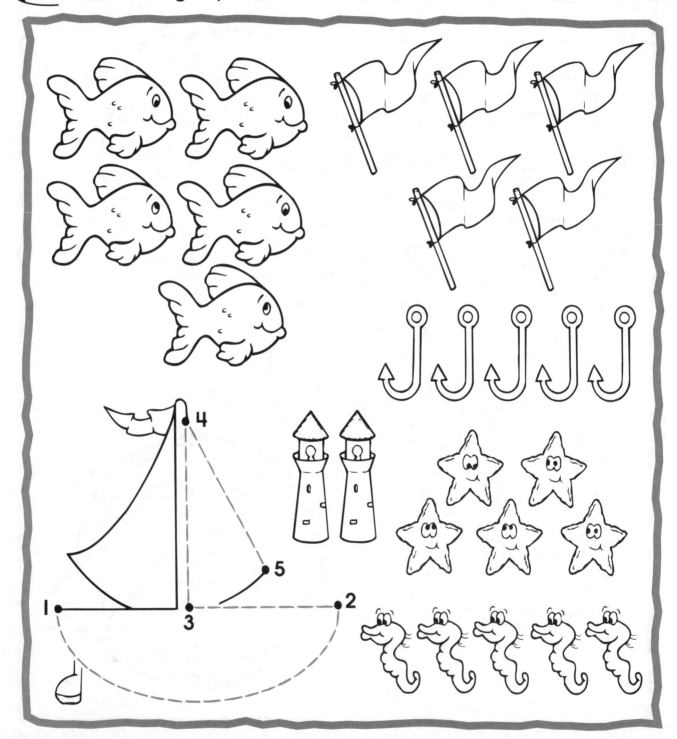

Name_____

Trace the Numbers

Trace the numbers and words. Practice **writing** the numbers on the line below.

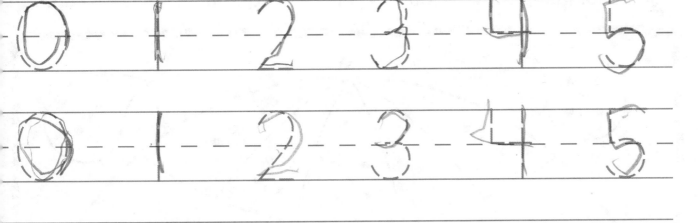

0 1 2 3 4 5

0 1 2 3 4 5

zero zero one

one two two

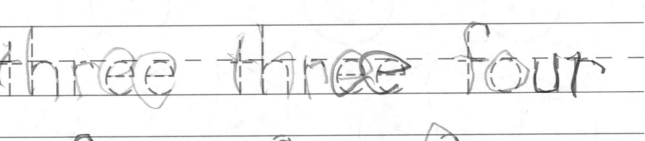

three three four

four five five

Name _____

Count the Dots

Count the dots.

| 1 • | 2 •• | 3 ⋮ | 4 ∷ | 5 ∷• |

Color the spaces: **1** - red   **2** - yellow   **3** - green   **4** - blue   **5** - orange

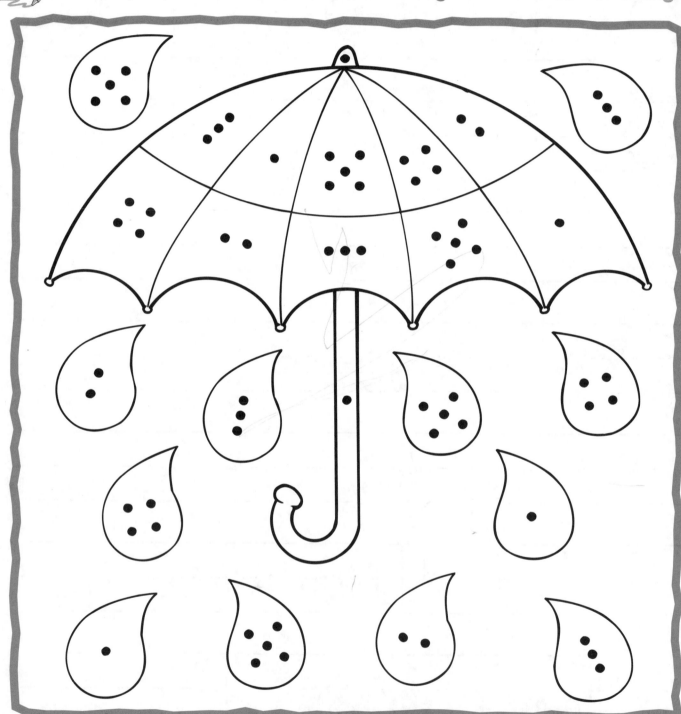

Name _____

How Many?

Trace the correct number for each box. **Color** all the pictures.

Name_____

Count the Pictures

Count each set of pictures.

 Write the number in the boxes below. **Color** the pictures.

How many?

Name_____

Color the Spaces

Color the spaces: **1 - red   2 - blue   3 - yellow   4 - green   5 - orange**

Name_____

Trace the Dotted Line

Trace the dotted line from **1–5** on each picture. **Color** the picture.

Name _____

Count Each Group

Count each group of vegetables.    **Write** the number in the box.
Color the vegetables, too.

0 1 2 3 4 5

How many? ☐

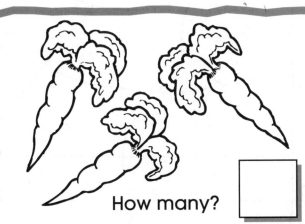

How many? ☐

How many? ☐

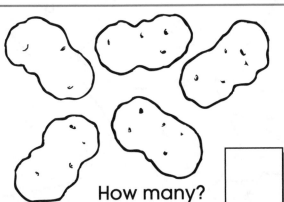

How many? ☐

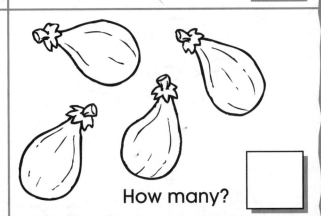

How many? ☐

Name_____

Color the Spaces

Color the spaces: **1** - blue   **2** - yellow   **3** - green   **4** - red   **5** - purple

What is it?

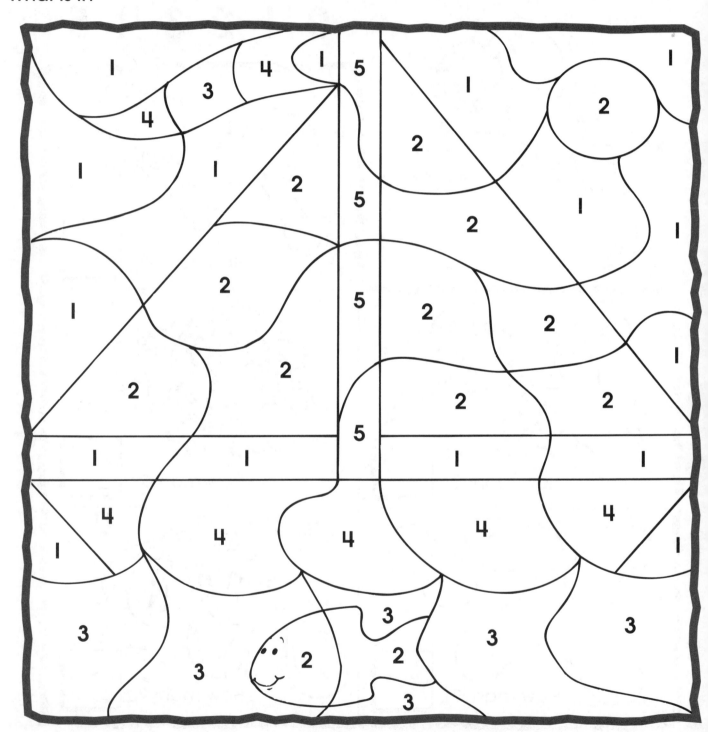

Name_____

Trace the Dotted Line

✏️ **Trace** the dotted line from **1–5**.

Color the picture. 🖍️

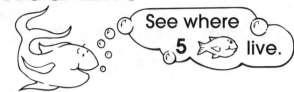

See where 5 🐟 live.

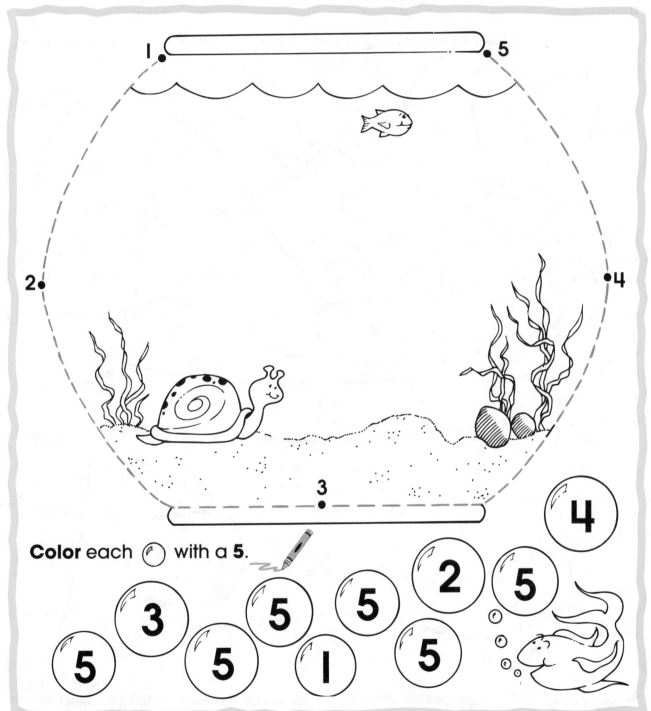

Color each ⚬ with a **5**. 🖍️

Name_____

Color the Spaces

Color the spaces: **5** - **white**   ⠿ - **black**   **five** - **red**   **4** - *pink*
3 - *yellow*   **2** - **blue**

What is it?

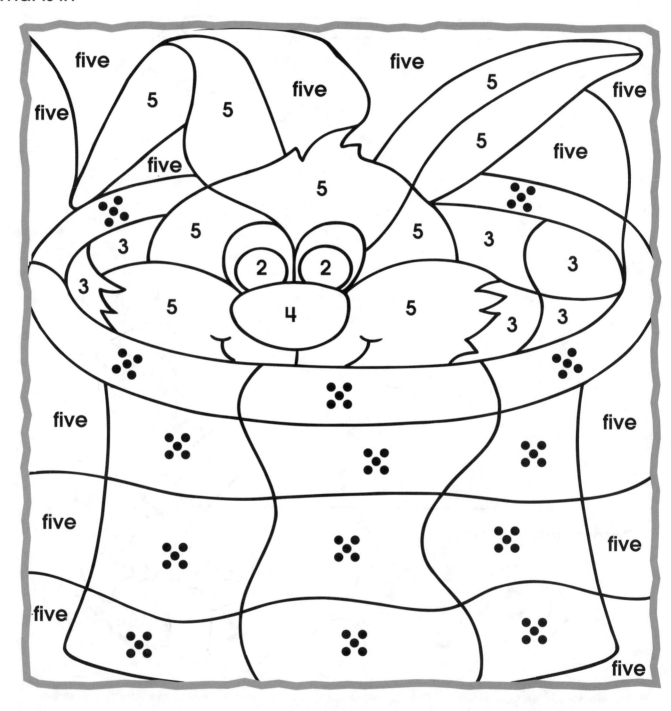

Name_____

Trace the Dotted Line

Trace the dotted line from **one** to **five**. **Color** the picture.

What is it?

Name_____

Count the Pictures

Count the pictures. **Trace** the numbers and the words. **Draw** a line to match.

1 one

2 two

3 three

4 four

5 five

Name _____

Circle the Number Words

Circle the number words in the puzzle. The first one is done for you.

Color the picture.

zero
one
two
three
four
five

f	e	o	f	i	v	e
t	h	r	e	e	b	t
x	o	n	e	s	i	w
f	o	u	r	a	d	e
z	e	r	o	t	w	o

Name_____

How Many?

Circle the correct number in each box. **Color** the pictures.

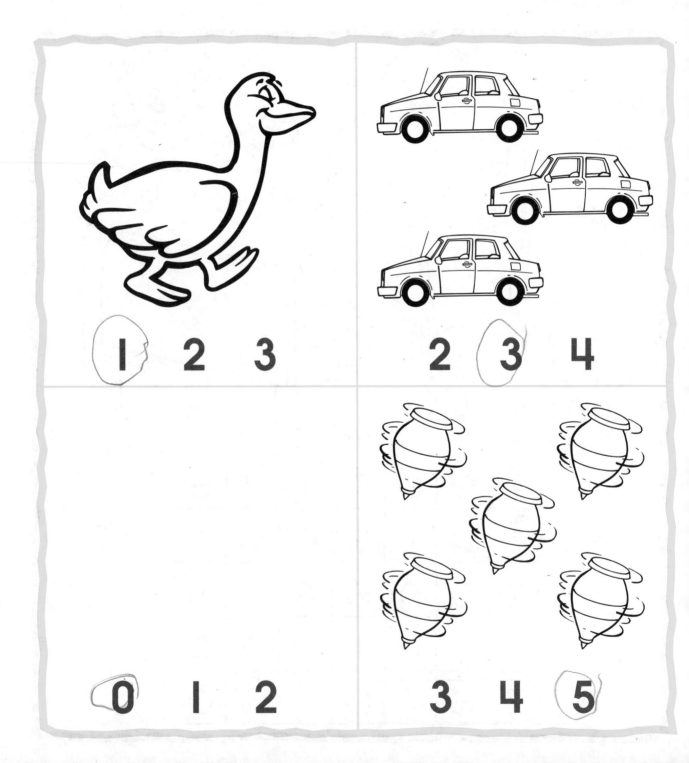

Name_____

How Many?

2 3 4

3 4 5

1 2 3

3 4 5

3 4 5

1 2 3

Name_____

Look at the Picture

How many do you see? ____ **Write** the number in the box.

Color the picture.

Name_____

Number 6

Color the number. **Color** the word. **Color** the rest of the picture.

Trace 6

✎ **Trace** the number.

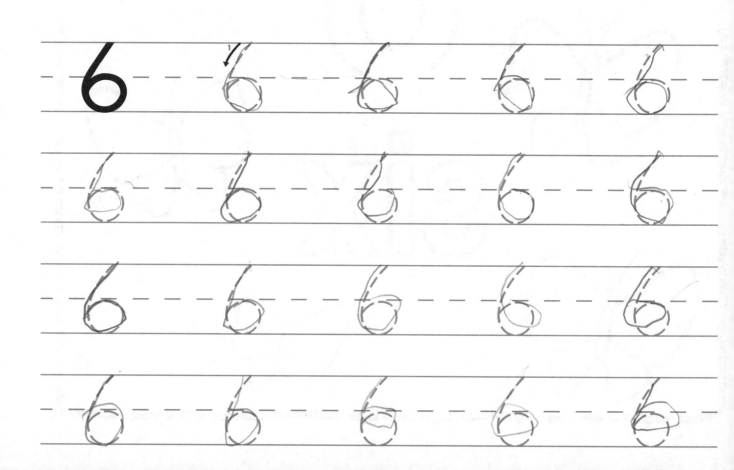

Name_____

Trace Six

✏️ **Trace** the word.

six

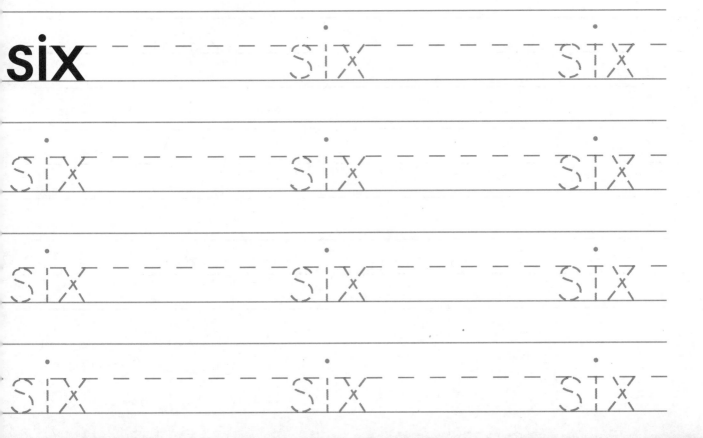

Name_____

Write 6

Now practice **writing** the number by yourself on the lines below.

Name_____

Write Six

Now practice **writing** the word by yourself on the lines below.

six

six

six

Name_____

Count and Color 6

 **Count** and **color** each group of pictures.

Trace the dotted line from **1–6**. **Circle** each group of **6**.

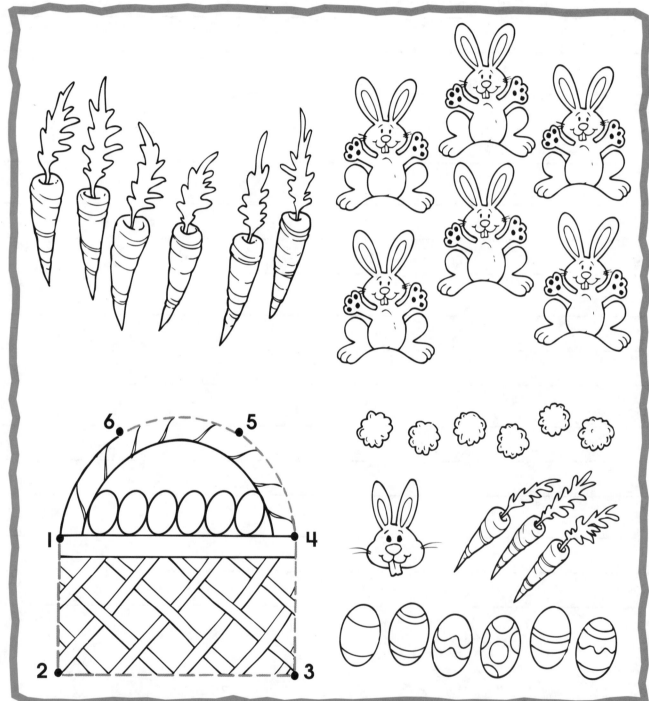

Name _____

Pop a Snack

Pop a snack!

Color the spaces: **6 - white**    **- yellow**   **six - green**   **5 - red**

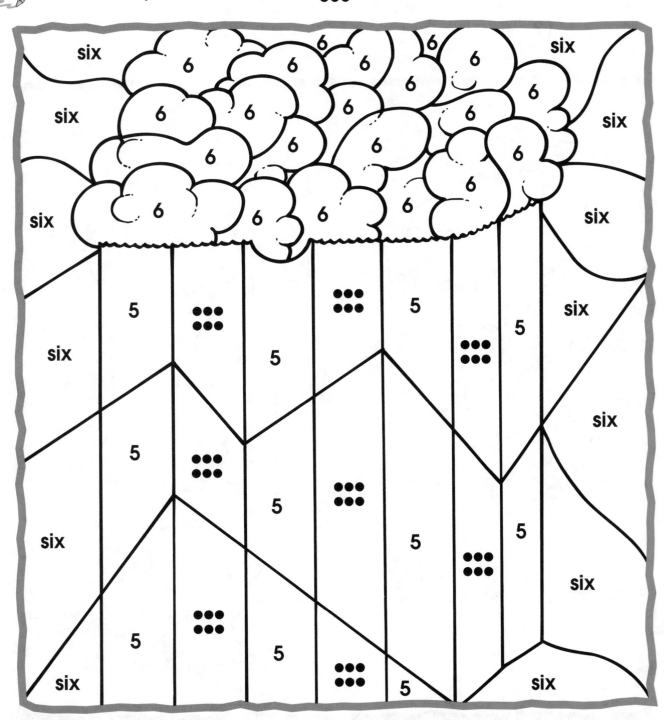

Name_____

Where are the 6's?

Where are the **6's**?

Circle the **6's**. **Color** the picture.

How many 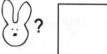? ☐

Name_____

Number 7

Color the number. **Color** the word. **Color** the rest of the picture.

Name_____

Trace 7

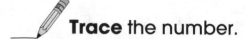 **Trace** the number.

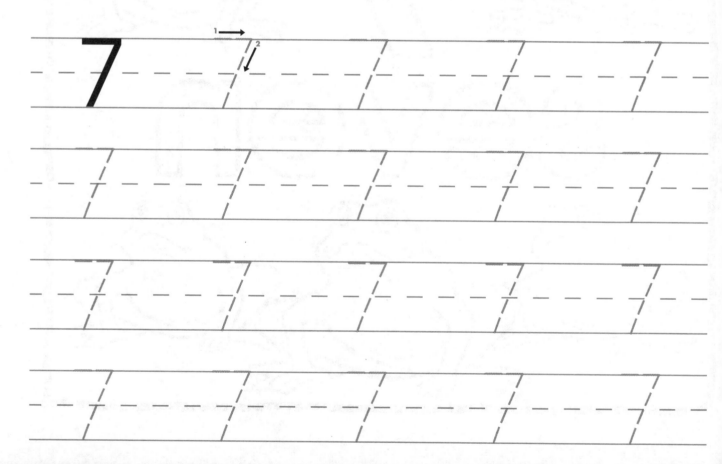

Name _____

Trace Seven

✎ **Trace** the word.

seven

seven seven seven
seven seven seven
seven seven seven
seven seven seven

Name_____

Write 7

Now practice **writing** the number by yourself on the lines below.

Name_____

Write Seven

Now practice **writing** the word by yourself on the lines below.

seven

seven

seven

Name_____

Where are the 7's?

Where are the **7's**?

Circle the **7's**. **Color** the picture.

How many ? ☐

Name_____

Count and Color 7

Count and **color** each group of pictures.

Trace the dotted line from **1–7**.   Circle each group of **7**.

Name_____

Trace the Dotted Line

Trace the dotted line from **1–7**.
Draw 7 apples on the tree.

It's heaven, when I find **7**.

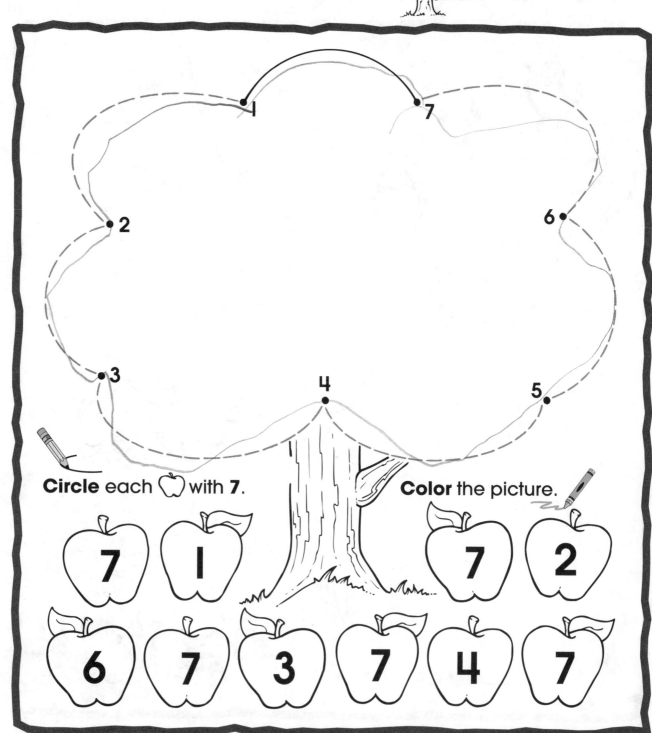

Circle each 🍎 with **7**.

Color the picture.

7   1

7   2

6   7   3   7   4   7

Name_____

Number 8

Color the number. **Color** the word. **Color** the rest of the picture.

Trace 8

Trace the number.

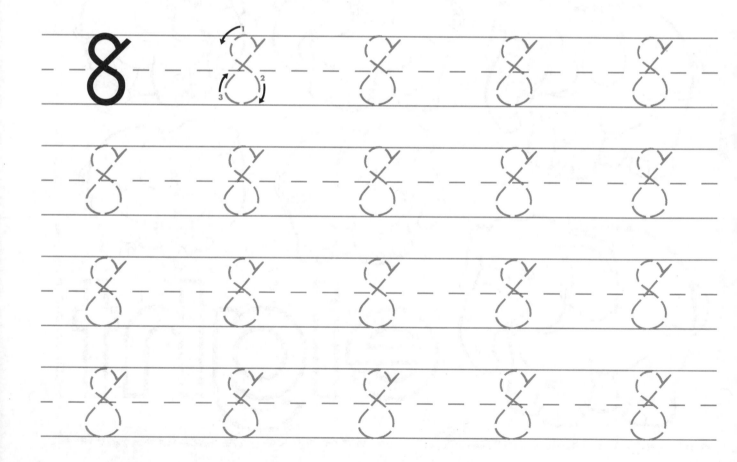

Name_____

Trace Eight

✏️ **Trace** the word.

eight

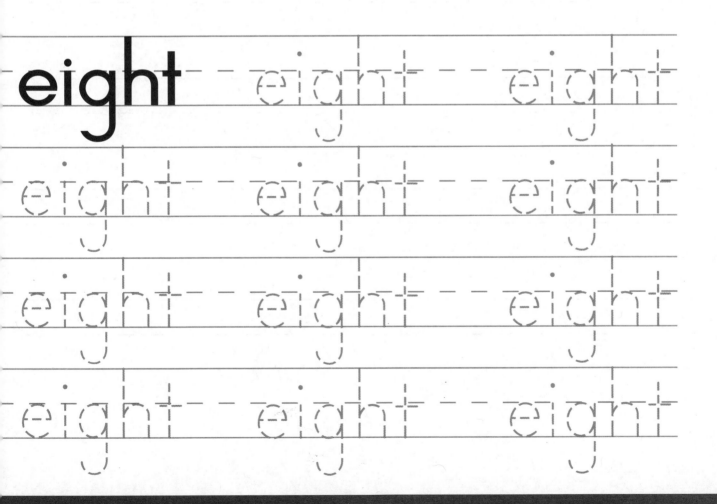

Name_____

Write 8

Now practice **writing** the number by yourself on the lines below.

Name _____

Write Eight

Now practice **writing** the word by yourself on the lines below.

Name_____

Color 8

 Color the spaces: **8** - yellow ▓▓▓ - red **eight** - green

What is it?

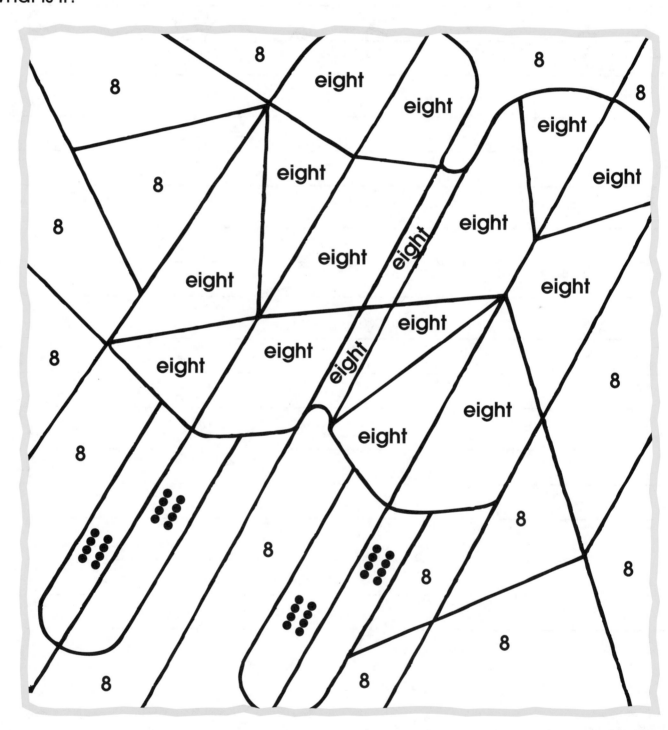

Name _____

Draw 8

Draw 8 s on the . **Color** the picture.

Name_____

Number 9

Color the number. **Color** the word. **Color** the rest of the picture.

Name _____

Trace 9

Trace the number.

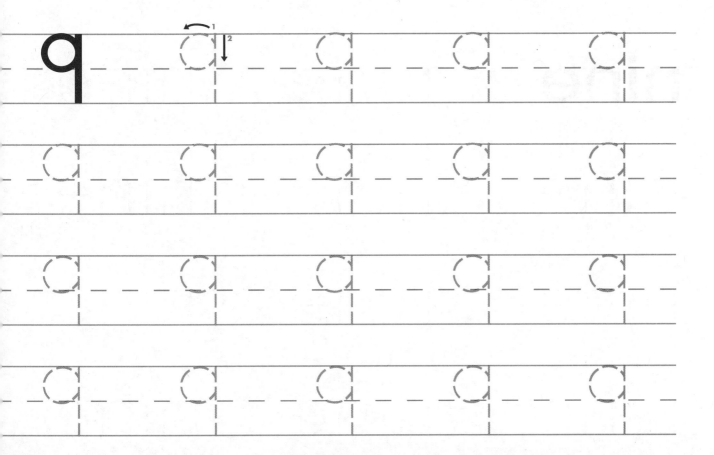

Name_____

Trace Nine

 **Trace** the word.

nine

Name _____

Write 9

Now practice **writing** the number by yourself on the lines below.

Name_____

Write Nine

Now practice **writing** the word by yourself on the lines below.

nine

nine

nine

Name_____

Count and Color 9

Count and **color** each picture.

Trace the dotted lines from **1–9**.

Circle each group of **9**.

Name_____

Color 9

 Color the spaces: **9** - white ●●●● - blue **nine** - red

What is it?

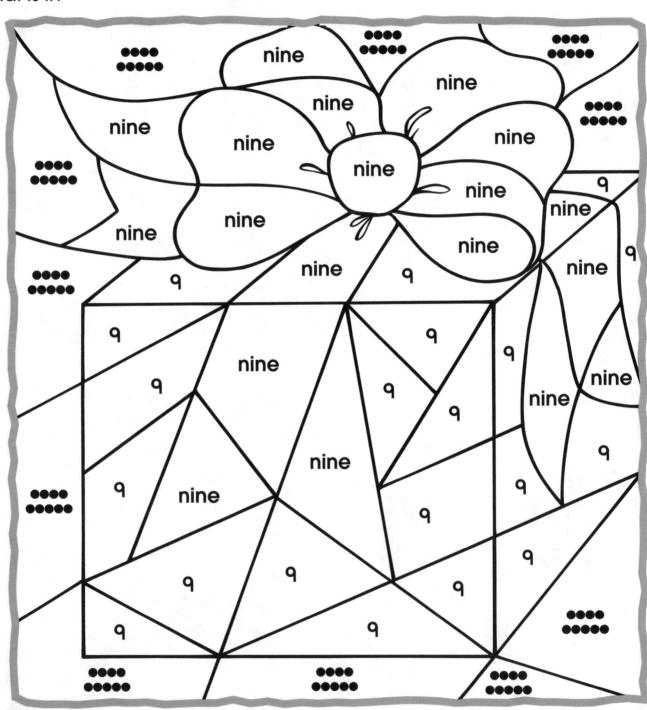

Name_____

Number 10

Color the number. **Color** the word. **Color** the rest of the picture.

Name _____

Trace 10

✏️ **Trace** the number.

10

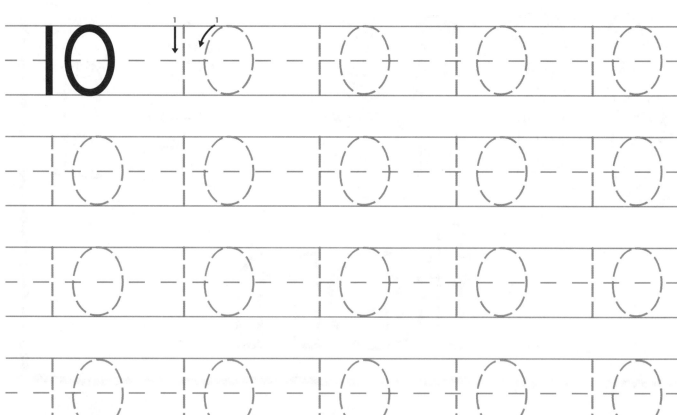

Name _____

Trace Ten

✏️ **Trace** the word.

ten

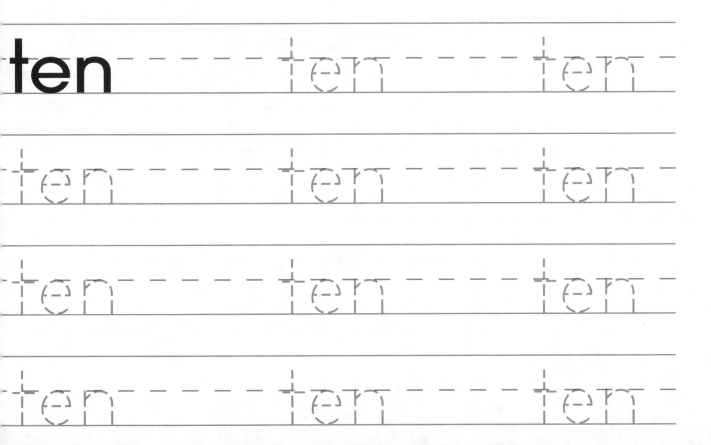

Write 10

Now practice **writing** the number by yourself on the lines below.

Name_____

Write Ten

Now practice **writing** the word by yourself on the lines below.

ten

ten

ten

Name_____

Draw 10

 Draw 10 s on this shirt. **Color** the picture.

Name_____

Where are the 10's?

Where are the **10's**?

Circle the **10's**. **Color** the picture.

How many 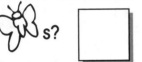s?

Name_____

Trace and Write the Numbers

Trace and **write** the numbers and the words. Practice writing the numbers on the lines below.

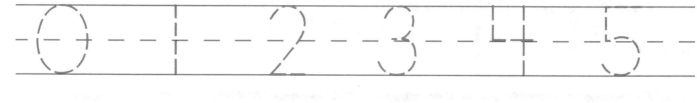

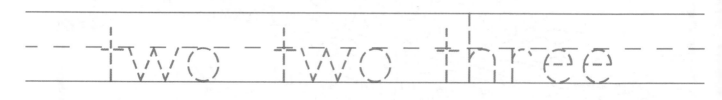

Name_____

Trace and Write the Numbers

Trace and **write** the numbers and the words. Practice writing the numbers on the lines below.

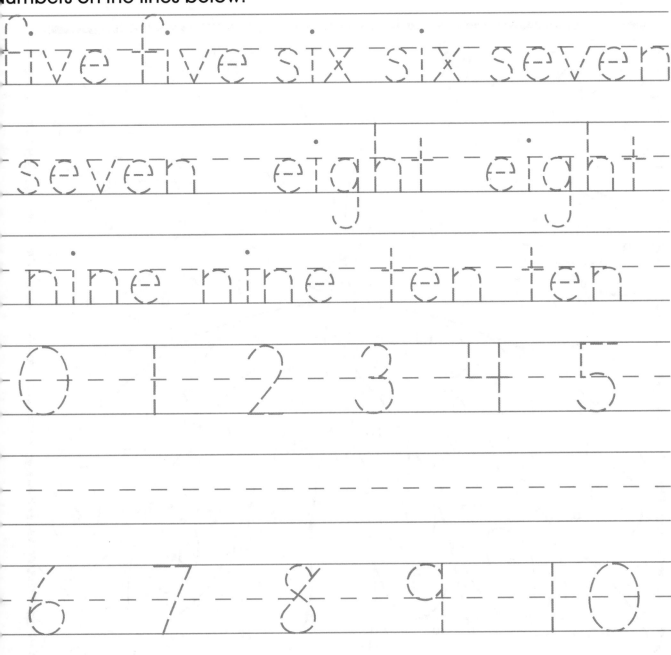

Name_____

Color the Spaces

Color the spaces: **6's** - red   **7's** - blue   **8's** - yellow   **9's** - green
10's - orange

Name_____

Write the Matching Number

ead each number word. **Write** the matching number on the cone.

0 1 2 3 4 5 6 7 8 9 10

seven   nine   two   five

three   ten   six

zero   one   eight   four

Name_____

Color the Correct Number

Color the correct number of things in each row.

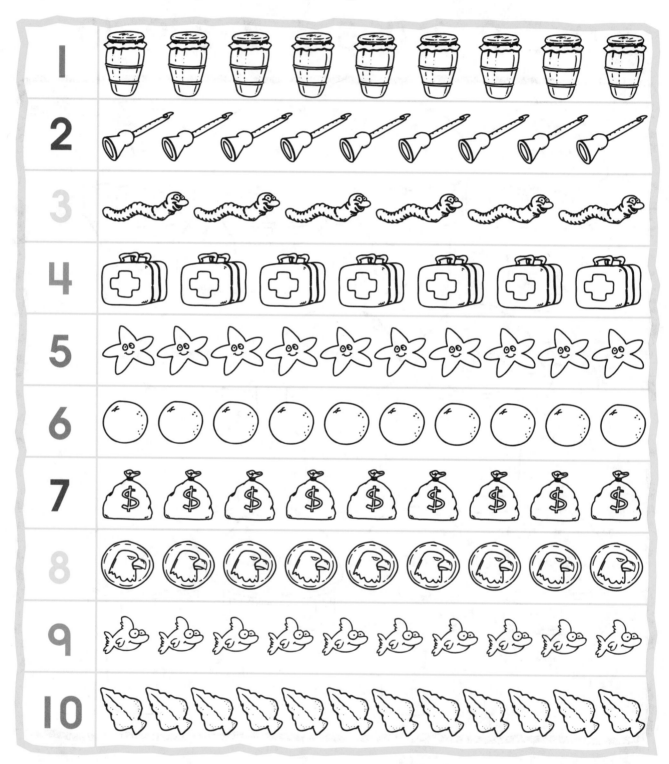

Name _____

Too Many Objects

Too many objects!

✏ **Draw** an **X** on the extra objects in each group.

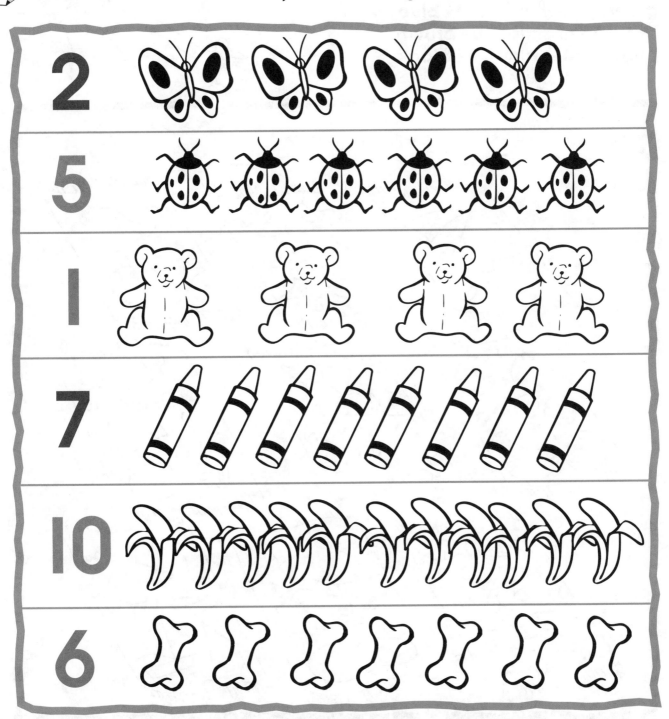

Name _____

Count and Color

Count. Use the code to **color** the pictures to match the number on each towel.

1 - green   2 - yellow   3 - blue
4 - red   5 - orange   6 - brown
7 - purple   8 - gray   9 - black

Name_____

Color the Marbles

Color the correct number of marbles in each bag.

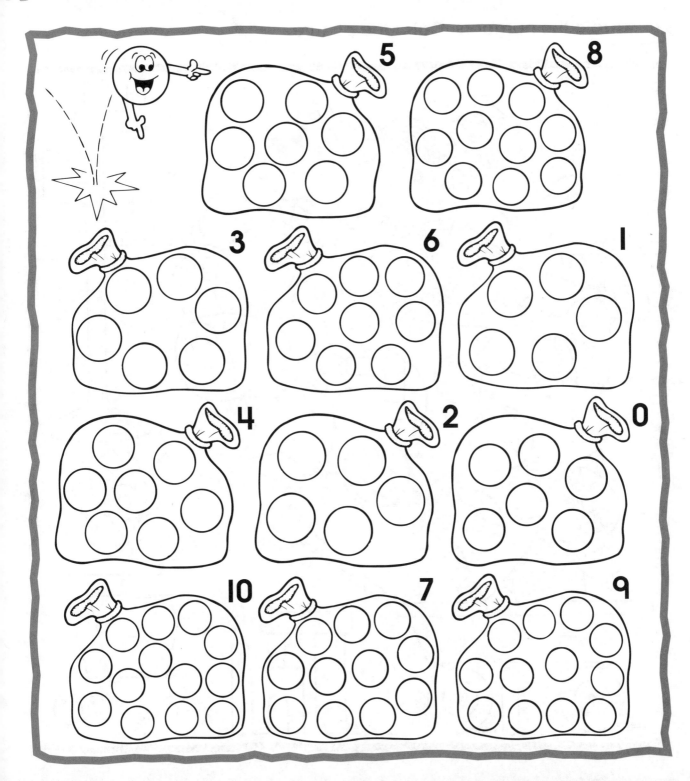

Name_____

Find the Hidden Numbers

Find the hidden numbers **0-10**.

Circle the numbers. **Color** the picture.

Name_____

Draw a Line

Draw a line from each to the correct number word.

three
six
one
seven
two
five
ten
eight
nine
four

Name_____

Count Each Group

Count each group of animals. _____ **Draw** a line from the number to the correct number word. The first one is done for you.

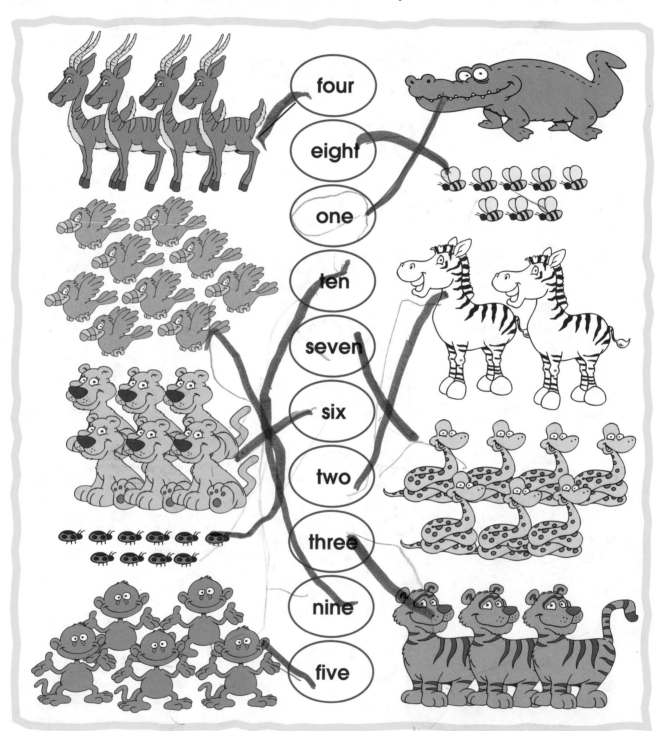

Name_____

Connect the Dots

Connect the dots in order from 1–10. Color the picture.

What is it?

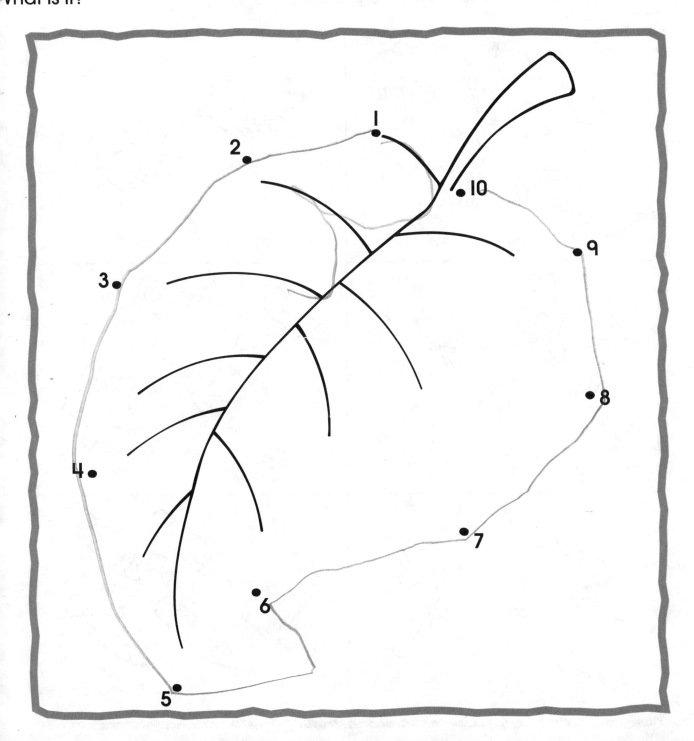

Name_____

Count the Pictures

Count the pictures in each group.

 Circle the number. **Color** the pictures.

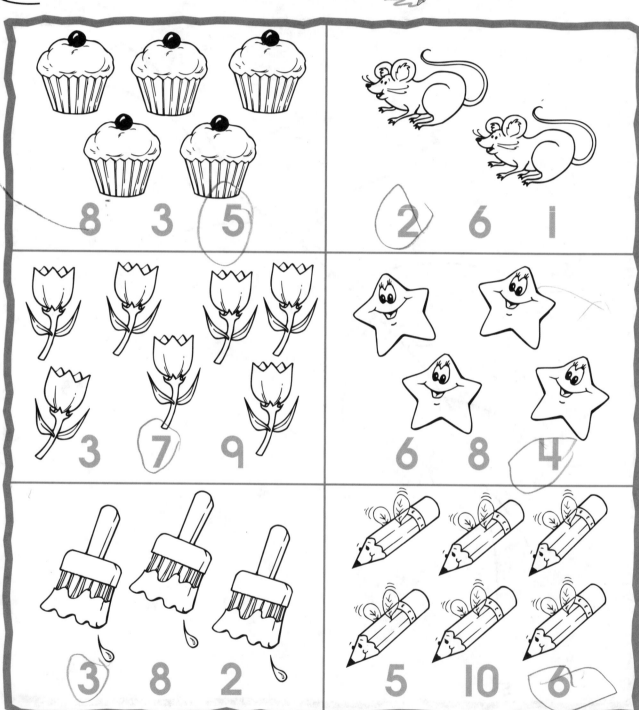

Name_____

Trace the Dotted Line

Trace the dotted line from **1-10**. **Draw** and **color** a picture on Teddy's shirt.

1 2 3 4 5 6 7 8 9 10

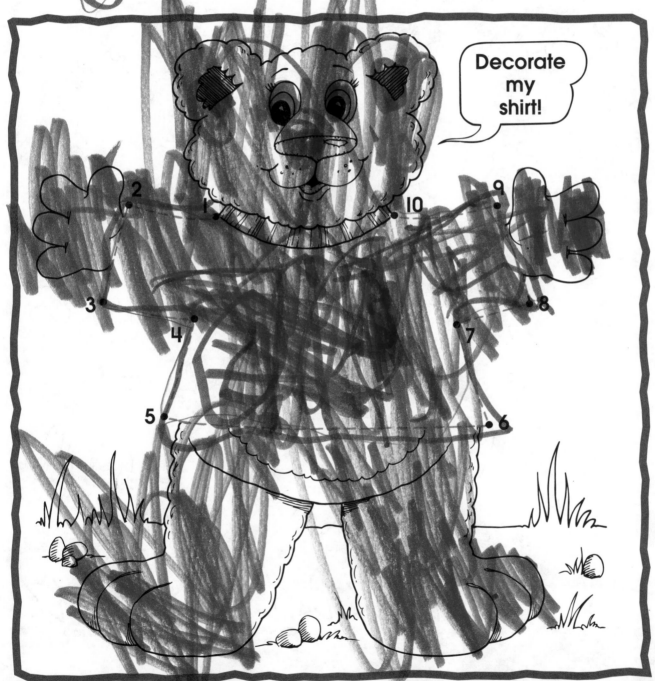

Decorate my shirt!

Name_____

Color the Number

Color the number. **Color** the correct number of objects in each row.

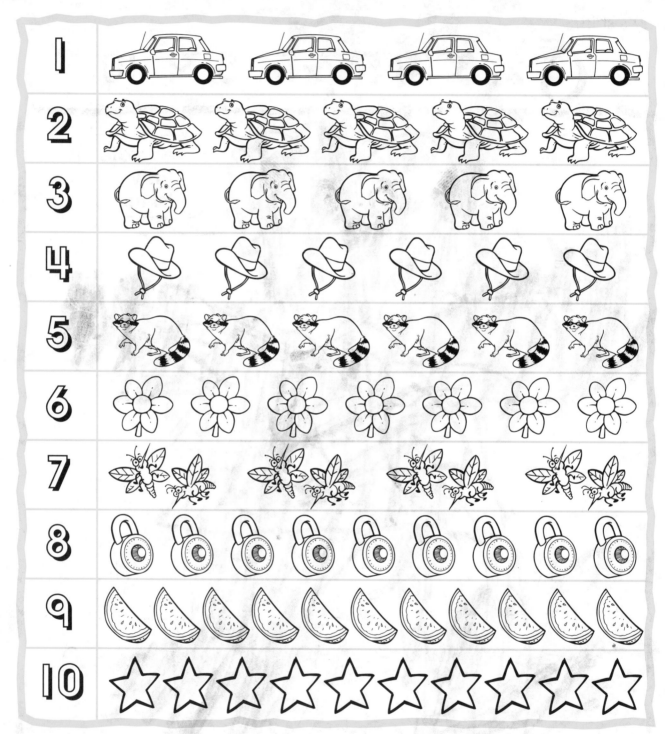

Name_____

Count the Dots

Count the dots.

| 6 | ⦙⦙⦙ | 7 | ⦙⦙⦙⦙ | 8 | ⦙⦙⦙⦙ | 9 | ⦙⦙⦙⦙⦙ | 10 | ⦙⦙⦙⦙⦙ |

Color the spaces: **6 - purple**   **7 - green**   **8 - orange**   **9 - blue**

10 - yellow

Name_____

Write the Missing Numbers

Write the missing numbers on each pencil.

1 2 3 4 5 6 7 8 9 10

Name_____

Count the Pictures

Count the pictures in each group.

Circle the number. Color the pictures.

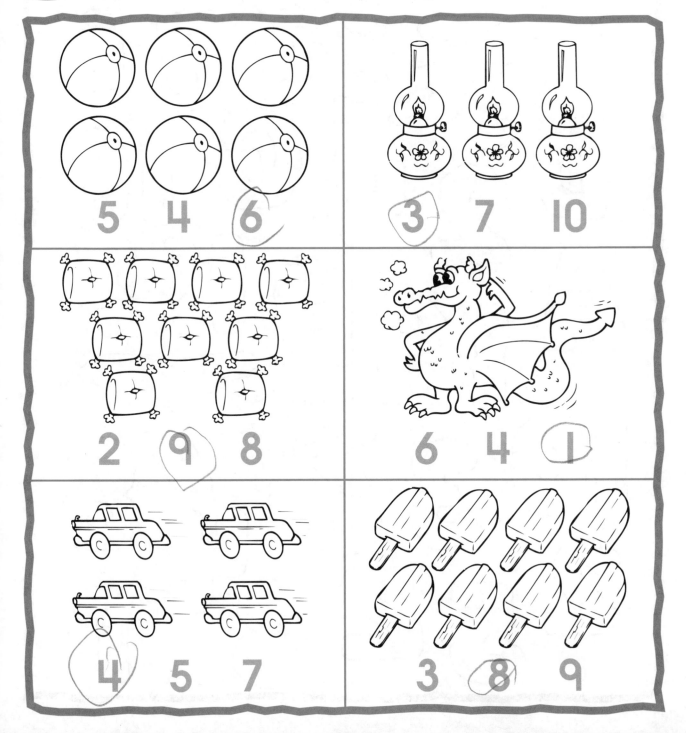

Name_____

Color Each Number

Color each number.　　**Draw** an **X** on each letter.

Name_____

Circle the Number Words

Circle the number words in the puzzle. Look ⟶ and ↓.

zero	four	eight
one	five	nine
two	six	ten
three	seven	

t	a	f	o	u	r	z
w	s	e	v	e	n	e
o	c	n	i	n	e	r
o	n	e	t	e	n	o
g	e	i	g	h	t	s
b	f	i	v	e	v	i
f	t	h	r	e	e	x

Name_____

Count the Number of Each Thing

Count the number of each thing in the picture. **Write** the number on the line.

Name_____

Count the Sheep

ount the sheep on the hill. ✏️ Then, **write** that number on each tree.

Name_____

Number 11

Color the number. **Color** the word. **Color** the rest of the picture.

Name _____

Trace 11

Trace the number.

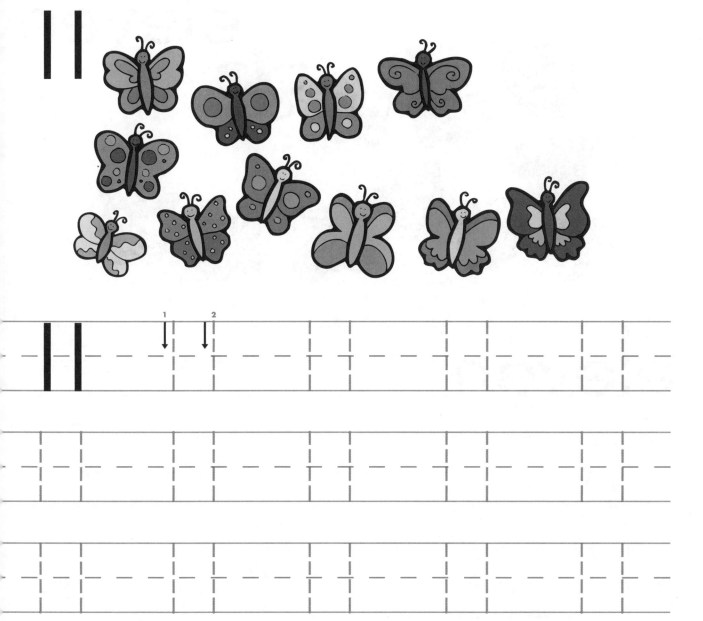

Name_____

Trace Eleven

Trace the word.

eleven

eleven

eleven   eleven

eleven   eleven

eleven   eleven

eleven   eleven

Name_____

Write 11

Now practice **writing** the number by yourself on the lines below.

Name_____

Write Eleven

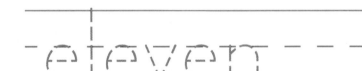 Now practice **writing** the word by yourself on the lines below.

eleven

eleven

eleven

Name_____

Ellie the Elephant

Ellie the Elephant juggles all day long.

Draw and **color** 11 balls for Ellie to juggle today. Don't forget to **color** Ellie, too!

Name_____

Number 12

Color the number. **Color** the word. **Color** the rest of the picture.

Name_____

Trace 12

✏ **Trace** the number.

12

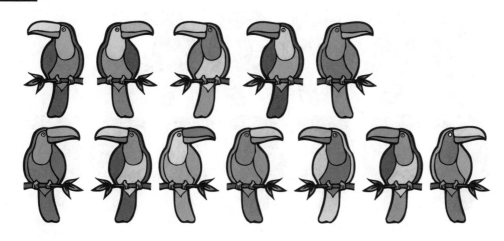

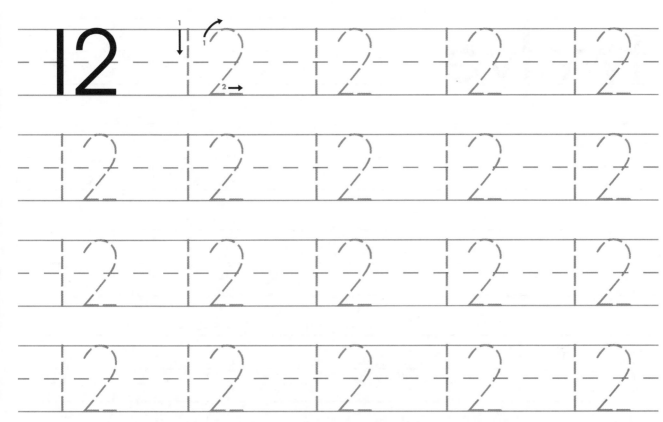

Name_____

Trace Twelve

Trace the word.

twelve

twelve   twelve

twelve   twelve

twelve   twelve

twelve   twelve

Name_____

Write 12

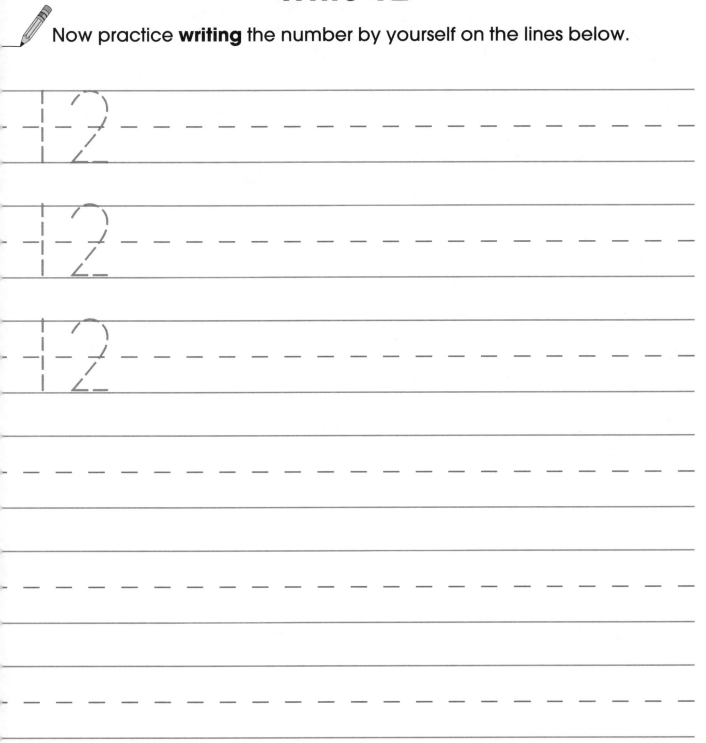

Now practice **writing** the number by yourself on the lines below.

Name_____

Write Twelve

Now practice **writing** the word by yourself on the lines below.

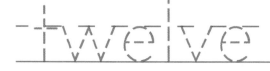

Name_____

Ted Turtle

Ted Turtle plays a terrific tune on his tuba.

Color 12 notes for Ted to play. **Color** Ted.

Name _____

Write the Missing Number

✏️ **Write** the missing numbers on each snake.

1 2 3 4 5 6 7 8 9 10 11 12

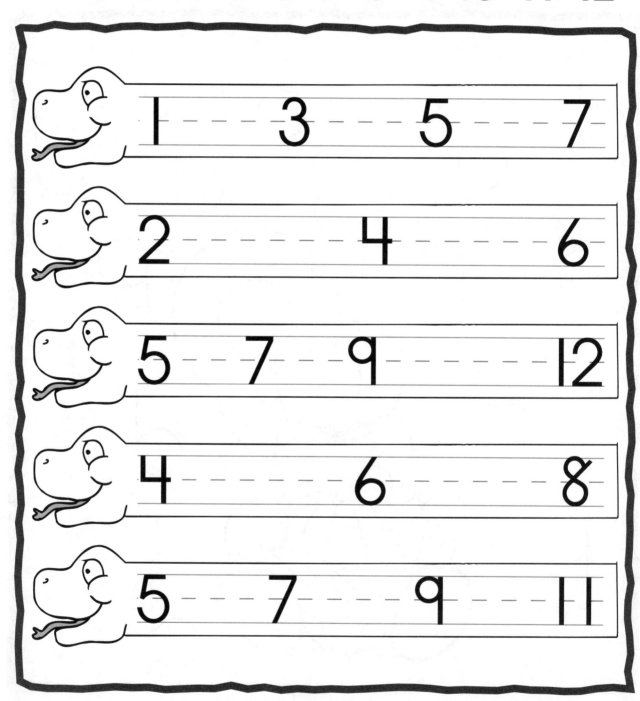

Name_____

Number 13

Color the number. **Color** the word. **Color** the rest of the picture.

Trace 13

✏ **Trace** the number.

13

13   13   13   13   13

13   13   13   13   13

13   13   13   13   13

13   13   13   13   13

Name_____

Trace Thirteen

✏️ **Trace** the word.

thirteen

thirteen

thirteen ----- thirteen

thirteen ----- thirteen

thirteen ----- thirteen

thirteen ----- thirteen

Name_____

Write 13

Now practice **writing** the number by yourself on the lines below.

13

13

13

Name_____

Write Thirteen

 Now practice **writing** the word by yourself on the lines below.

thirteen

thirteen

thirteen

Name_____

Draw 13

 Draw 13 donuts in the bakery box.

Color the donuts to match your favorite flavors.

Name_____

Number 14

Color the number. **Color** the word. **Color** the rest of the picture.

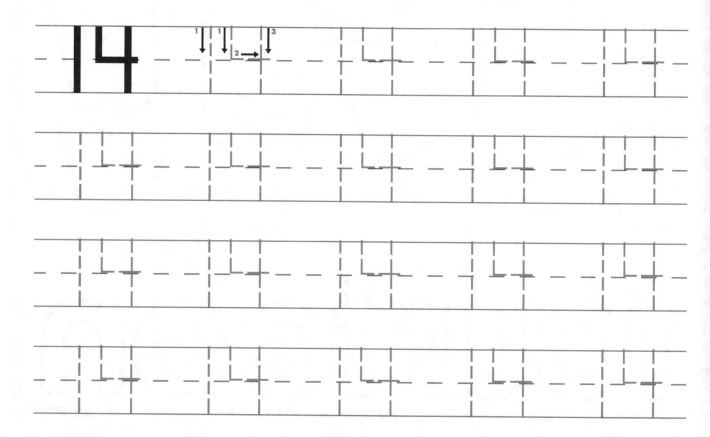

Name_____

Trace 14

✎ **Trace** the number.

14

Name_____

Trace Fourteen

Trace the word.

fourteen

fourteen

fourteen fourteen

fourteen fourteen

fourteen fourteen

fourteen fourteen

Name_____

Write 14

Now practice **writing** the number by yourself on the lines below.

Name_____

Write Fourteen

Now practice **writing** the word by yourself on the lines below.

fourteen

fourteen

fourteen

Name_____

Circle the Correct Number

How many?

 Circle the correct number for each box.

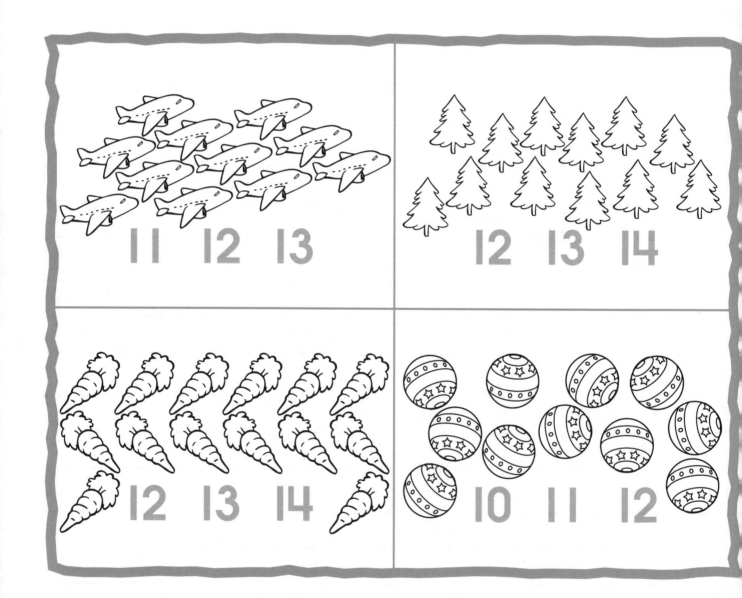

Name_____

Circle the Correct Number

How many?

✏️ **Circle** the correct number for each box.

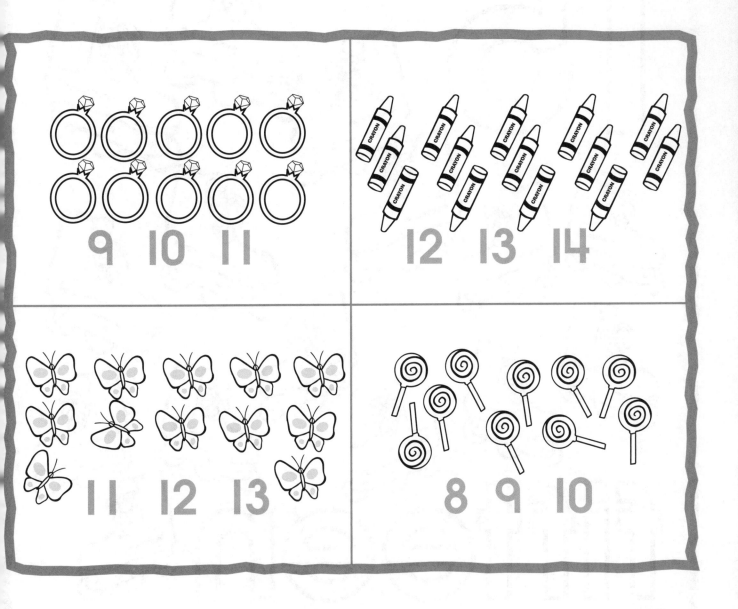

Name_____

Number 15

Color the number. **Color** the word. **Color** the rest of the picture.

Name_____

Trace the Number

✏️ **Trace** the number.

15

15

Name_____

Trace the Word

✏️ **Trace** the word.

fifteen

fifteen

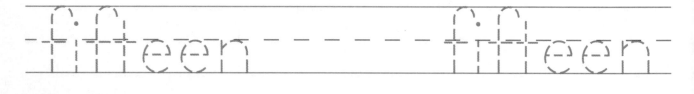

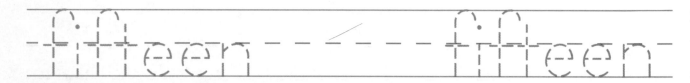

Name_____

Write 15

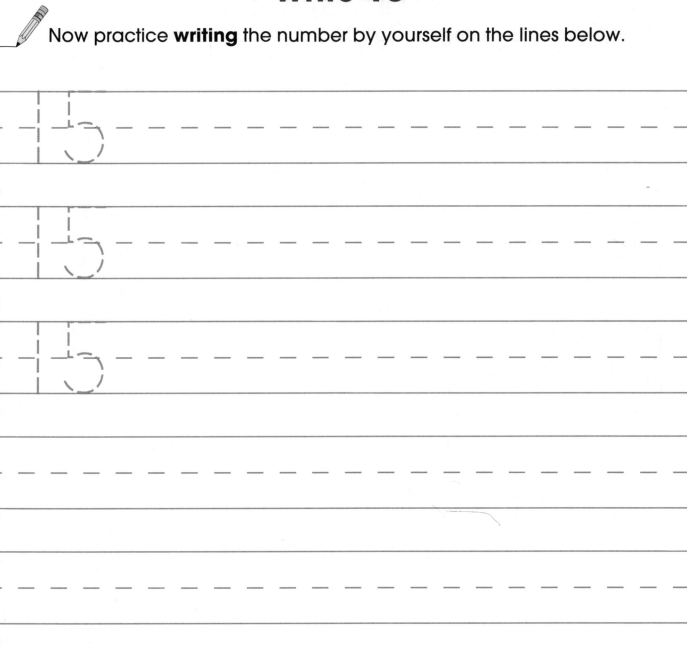

Now practice **writing** the number by yourself on the lines below.

Name_____

Write Fifteen

Now practice **writing** the word by yourself on the lines below.

fifteen

fifteen

fifteen

Name _____

Draw 15 Bows

Draw **15** bows on the tail of the kite!

Color the kite and bows with bright colors!

Name_____

Connect the Pawprints

Connect the feet in number order.

1 2 3 4 5 6 7 8 9 10 11 12 13 14 15

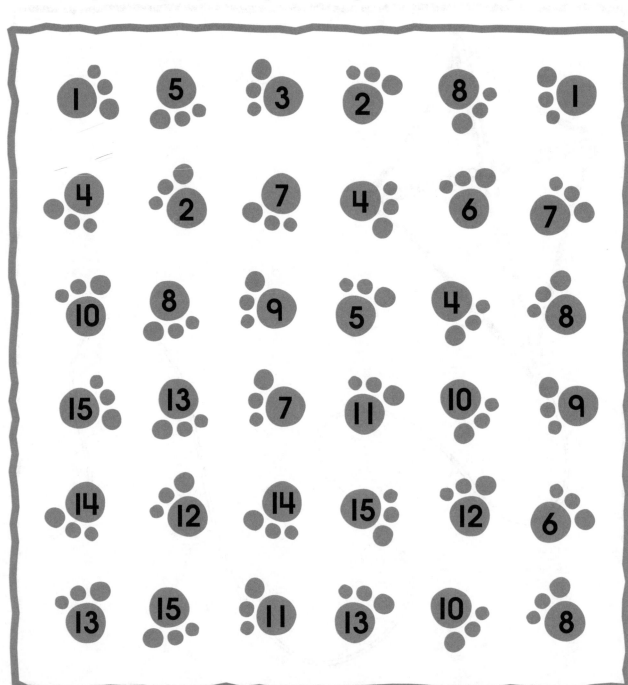

Name_____

Number 16

Color the number. **Color** the word. **Color** the rest of the picture.

Name_____

Trace 16

✏ **Trace** the number.

16

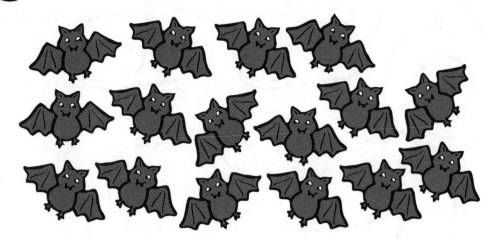

16 16 16 16 16

16 16 16 16 16

16 16 16 16 16

16 16 16 16 16

Name_____

Trace Sixteen

Trace the word.

sixteen

sixteen   sixteen

sixteen   sixteen

sixteen   sixteen

sixteen   sixteen

Name_____

Write 16

Now practice **writing** the number by yourself on the lines below.

Name_____

Write Sixteen

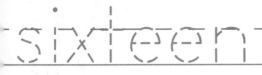 Now practice **writing** the word by yourself on the lines below.

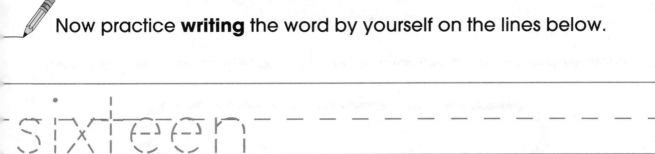

sixteen

sixteen

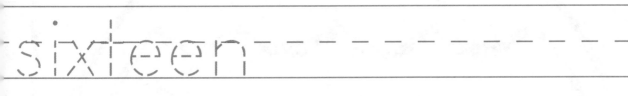

Name_____

Draw 16

Draw **16** fish in the fish bowl! **Color** the picture.

Name_____

Number 17

Color the number. **Color** the word. **Color** the rest of the picture.

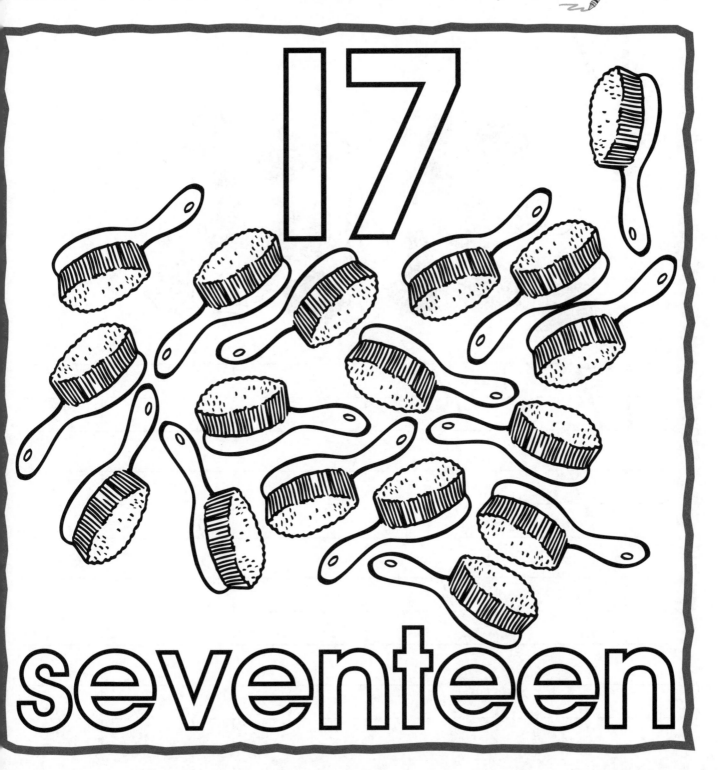

Name_____

Trace 17

✏️ **Trace** the number.

17

17 ⁷⁷↓ →₂

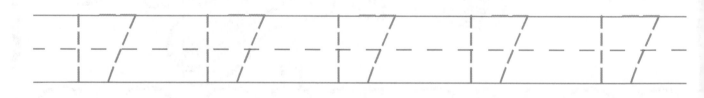

Name_____

Trace Seventeen

Trace the word.

seventeen

seventeen seventeen

seventeen seventeen

seventeen seventeen

seventeen seventeen

Name_____

Write 17

Now practice **writing** the number by yourself on the lines below.

Name_____

Write Seventeen

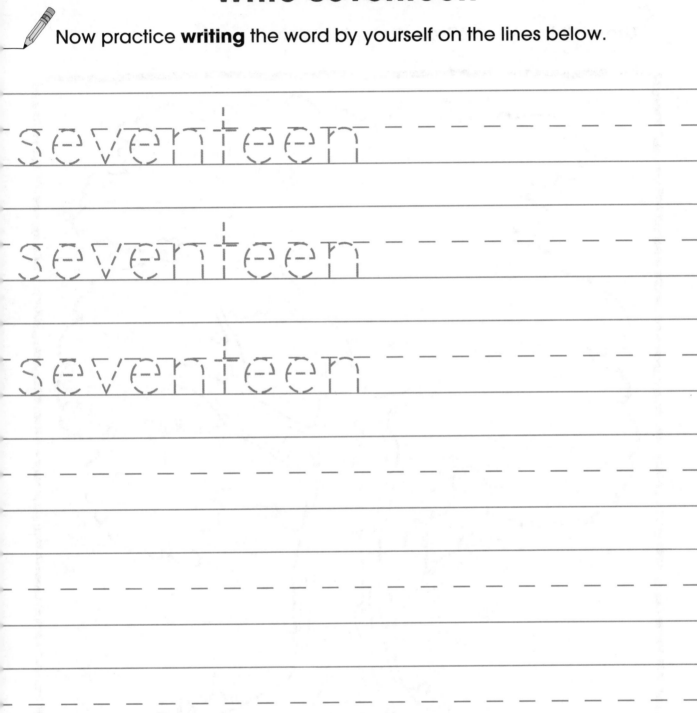

Now practice **writing** the word by yourself on the lines below.

seventeen

seventeen

seventeen

Name_____

Draw 17

✏️ **Draw 17** birds in the tree. **Color** the picture.

Name_____

Number 18

Color the number. **Color** the word. **Color** the rest of the picture.

Name_____

Trace 18

✏️ **Trace** the number.

18

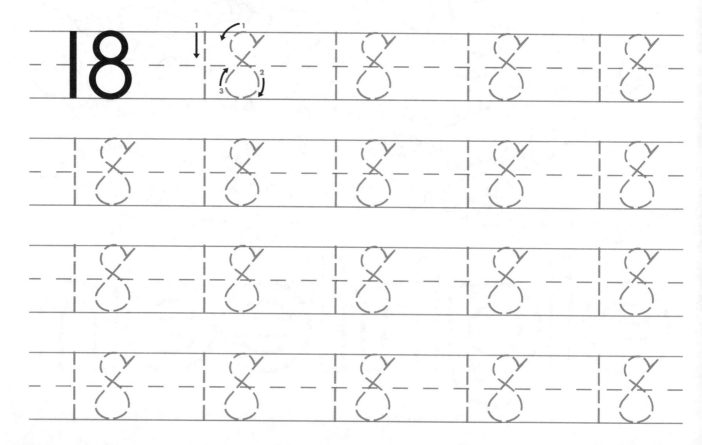

Name _____

Trace Eighteen

Trace the word.

eighteen

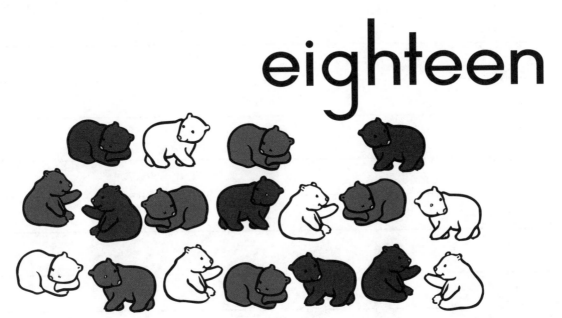

eighteen eighteen

eighteen eighteen

eighteen eighteen

eighteen eighteen

Name_____

Write 18

Now practice **writing** the number by yourself on the lines below.

Name _____

Write Eighteen

 Now practice **writing** the word by yourself on the lines below.

eighteen

eighteen

eighteen

Name_____

Draw 18

 Draw 18 s on the . **Color** the ⭐ s.

Name_____

Number 19

Color the number. **Color** the word. **Color** the rest of the picture.

Name_____

Trace 19

Trace the number.

1 9

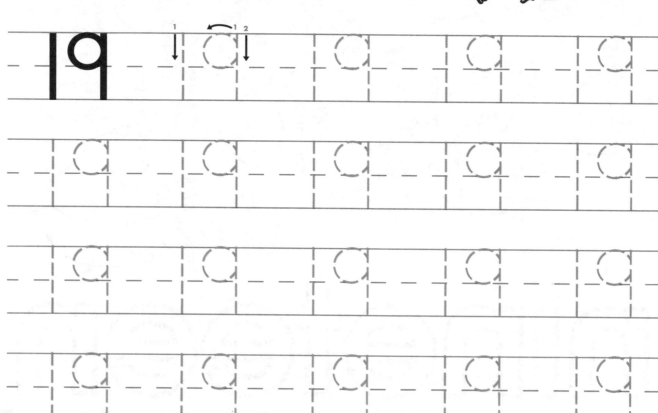

Name _____

Trace Nineteen

Trace the word.

nineteen

nineteen   nineteen

nineteen   nineteen

nineteen   nineteen

nineteen   nineteen

Name_____

Write 19

🖉 Now practice **writing** the number by yourself on the lines below.

Name_____

Write Nineteen

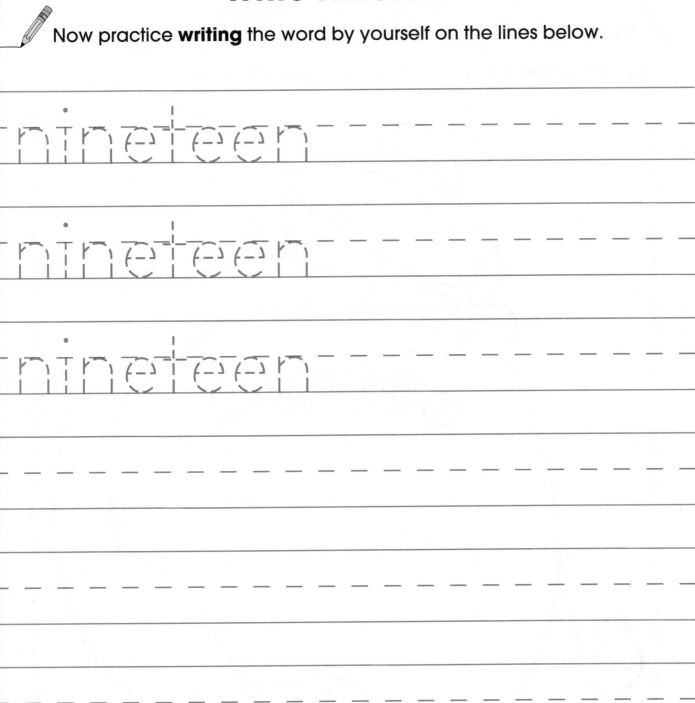

Now practice **writing** the word by yourself on the lines below.

nineteen

nineteen

nineteen

Name_____

Draw 19

Draw 19 cookies in the cookie jar. **Color** the picture.

Number 20

Color the number. **Color** the word. **Color** the rest of the picture.

Name_____

Trace 20

✏️ **Trace** the number.

20

20 20 20 20 20

20 20 20 20 20

20 20 20 20 20

20 20 20 20 20

Name _____

Trace Twenty

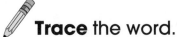 **Trace** the word.

twenty

twenty

twenty   twenty

twenty   twenty

twenty   twenty

twenty   twenty

Name_____

Write 20

Now practice **writing** the number by yourself on the lines below.

Name

Write Twenty

Now practice **writing** the word by yourself on the lines below.

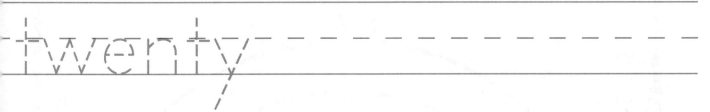

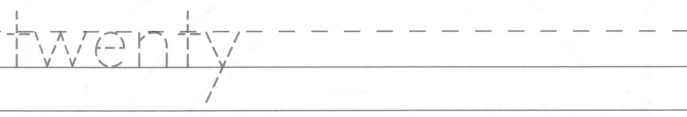

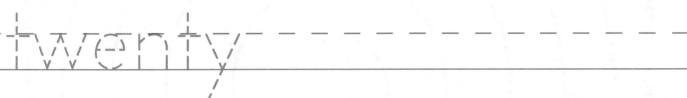

Name_____

Draw 20

 Draw 20 on the . **Color** the s.

Name _____

Practice 1-20

Trace the numbers and the words.

0   1   2   3   4

5   6   7   8   9

10   11   12   13

14   15   16   17

18   19   20

zero   one   two

three   four   five

Name_____

Trace the Number Words

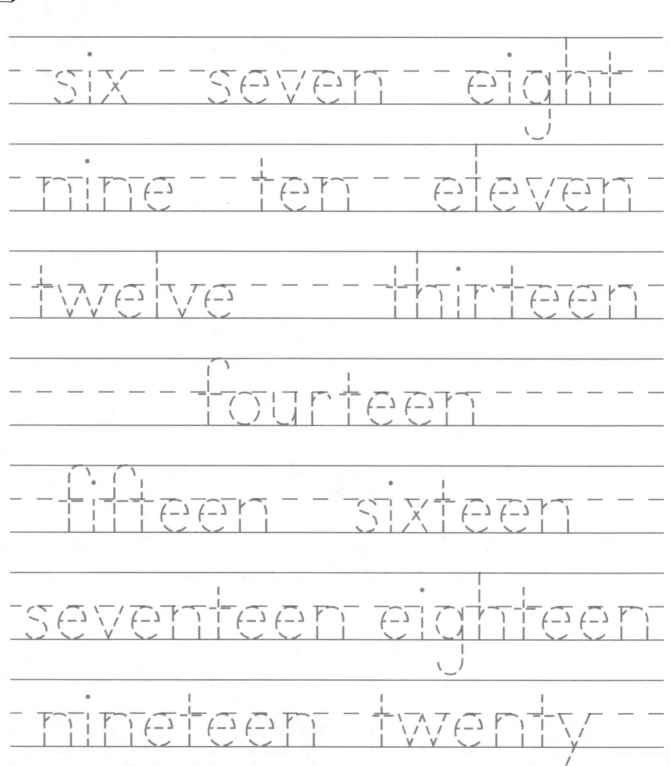

✏ **Trace** the number words.

six seven eight
nine ten eleven
twelve thirteen
fourteen
fifteen sixteen
seventeen eighteen
nineteen twenty

Name_____

Connect the Dots

Connect the dots in order from **1-12. Color** the picture.

Name_____

Connect the Dots

Connect the dots in order from **1–20. Color** the picture.

Name_____

Connect the Dots

Connect the dots in order from **1–20**. **Color** the surprise.

What is it?

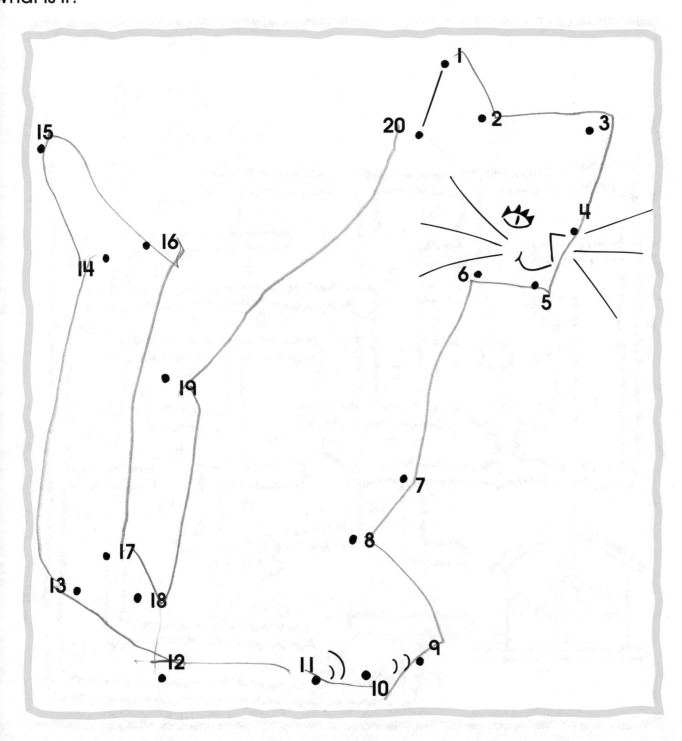

Name_____

Connect the Numbers

Connect the numbers in order from **0-20** to help the kitten find its home. **Color** the picture.

Name_____

Draw a Line

Draw a line from the word to the correct number.

even	1
wo	8
ive	3
hine	4
zero	7
six	5
our	6
one	2
hree	0
eight	9

Color the train cars: **1 - red   2 - blue   3 - green   4 - yellow
5 - orange   6 - brown**

Name_____

Count the Number

Count the number of each thing in the picture. **Write** the number in the correct box.

Name_____

Count the Number

Count the number of each thing in the picture. **Write** the number in the correct box.

Name_____

Count the Cats

Count the cats in each bed. **Write** the correct number of cats in the box on each bed.

Congratulations!

You know numbers **1–20**! **Color** this ribbon for everyone to see!

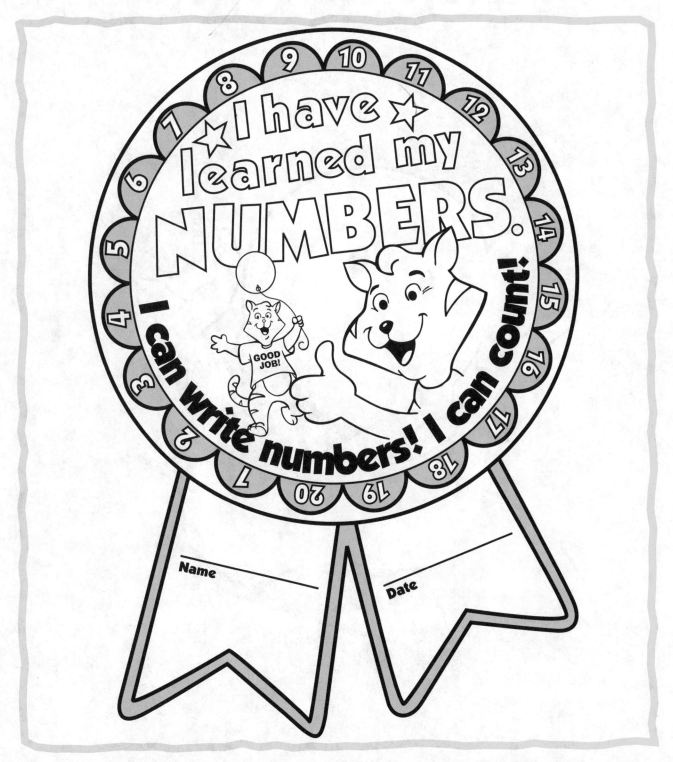

Place Value

Name_____

Circle Sets

Circle sets of ten marbles. **Count** how many tens and ones.

Write the number.

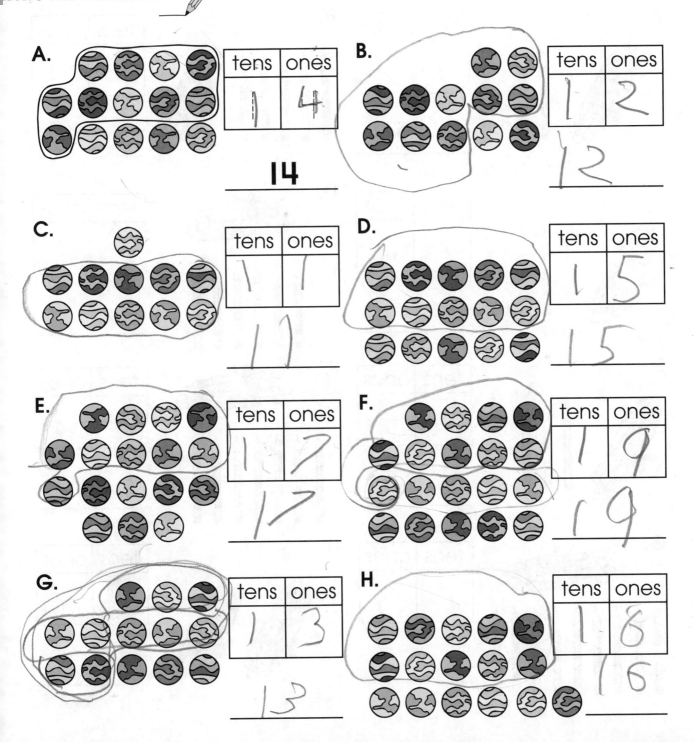

A.

tens	ones
1	4

14

B.

tens	ones
1	2

12

C.

tens	ones
1	1

11

D.

tens	ones
1	5

15

E.

tens	ones
1	7

17

F.

tens	ones
1	9

19

G.

tens	ones
1	3

13

H.

tens	ones
1	8

16

Name_____

Count How Many

Count how many tens and ones. ✏️ **Write** the number.

A.

tens	ones
1	2

12

B.

tens	ones
1	5

_____

C.

tens	ones
1	1

D.

tens	ones
1	6

_____

E.

tens	ones
1	3

F.

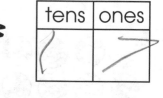

tens	ones
1	7

_____

G.

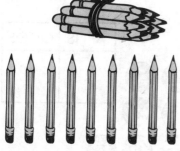

tens	ones
1	9

H.

tens	ones
2	0

_____

Name _____

Use the Numbers

Use the numbers on the left of the charts to **write** in the ones place to see how numbers **20–29** are made. The number in the tens place stays the same for all ten numbers.

	tens	ones
20	2	0

	tens	ones
21	2	

	tens	ones
22	2	

	tens	ones
23	2	

	tens	ones
24	2	

	tens	ones
25	2	

	tens	ones
26	2	

	tens	ones
27	2	

	tens	ones
28	2	

	tens	ones
29	2	

Name_____

Use the Numbers

Use the numbers on the left of the charts to **write** in the ones place to see how numbers **30–39** are made. The number in the tens place stays the same for all ten numbers.

	tens	ones
30	3	0

	tens	ones
35	3	5

	tens	ones
31	3	1

	tens	ones
36	3	6

	tens	ones
32	3	2

	tens	ones
37	3	7

	tens	ones
33	3	3

	tens	ones
38	3	8

	tens	ones
34	3	4

	tens	ones
39	3	9

Name_____

Use the Numbers

Use the numbers on the left of the charts to **write** in the ones place to see how numbers **40–49** are made. The number in the tens place stays the same for all ten numbers.

	tens	ones
40	4	0

	tens	ones
45	4	5

	tens	ones
41	4	1

	tens	ones
46	4	6

	tens	ones
42	4	2

	tens	ones
47	4	7

	tens	ones
43	4	3

	tens	ones
48	4	8

	tens	ones
44	4	4

	tens	ones
49	4	9

Name_____

Count the Numbers

Count the numbers from **1–50**.

1	2	3	4	5
6	7	8	9	10
11	12	13	14	15
16	17	18	19	20
21	22	23	24	25
26	27	28	29	30
31	32	33	34	35
36	37	38	39	40
41	42	43	44	45
46	47	48	49	50

Name_____

Connect the Dots

Connect the dots in order from **1–50**. **Color** the creature.

What is it?

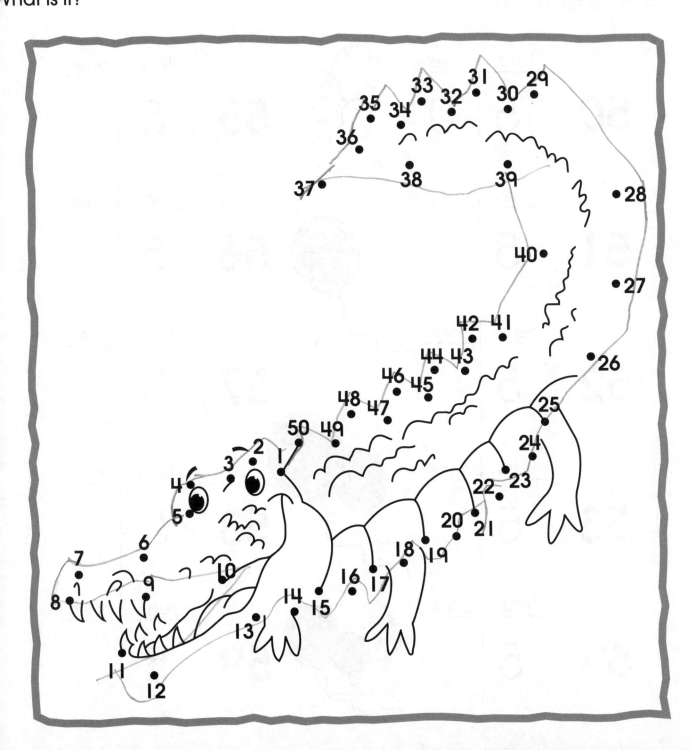

Name _____

Use the Numbers

Use the numbers on the left of the charts to **write** in the ones place to see how numbers **50–59** are made. The number in the tens place stays the same for all ten numbers.

	tens	ones
50	5	0

	tens	ones
55	5	

	tens	ones
51	5	

	tens	ones
56	5	

	tens	ones
52	5	

	tens	ones
57	5	

	tens	ones
53	5	

	tens	ones
58	5	

	tens	ones
54	5	

	tens	ones
59	5	

Name_____

Use the Numbers

Use the numbers on the left of the charts to **write** in the ones place to see how numbers **60-69** are made. The number in the tens place stays the same for all ten numbers.

	tens	ones
60	6	0

	tens	ones
61	6	1

	tens	ones
62	6	2

	tens	ones
63	6	3

	tens	ones
64	6	4

	tens	ones
65	6	5

	tens	ones
66	6	6

	tens	ones
67	6	7

	tens	ones
68	6	8

	tens	ones
69	6	9

Name_____

Use the Numbers

Use the numbers on the left of the charts to **write** in the ones place to see how numbers **70–79** are made. The number in the tens place stays the same for all ten numbers.

	tens	ones
70	7	0

	tens	ones
75	7	5

	tens	ones
71	7	1

	tens	ones
76	7	6

	tens	ones
72	7	

	tens	ones
77	7	7

	tens	ones
73	7	3

	tens	ones
78	7	

	tens	ones
74	7	4

	tens	ones
79	7	9

Name _____

Use the Numbers

Use the numbers on the left of the charts to **write** in the ones place to see how numbers **80-89** are made. The number in the tens place stays the same for all ten numbers.

	tens	ones
80	8	0

	tens	ones
85	8	5

	tens	ones
81	8	1

	tens	ones
86	8	6

	tens	ones
82	8	2

	tens	ones
87	8	7

	tens	ones
83	8	3

	tens	ones
88	8	8

	tens	ones
84	8	4

	tens	ones
89	8	9

Name_____

Use the Numbers

Use the numbers on the left of the charts to **write** in the ones place to see how numbers **90–99** are made. The number in the tens place stays the same for all ten numbers.

	tens	ones
90	9	0

	tens	ones
95	9	5

	tens	ones
91	9	1

	tens	ones
96	9	6

	tens	ones
92	9	2

	tens	ones
97	9	7

	tens	ones
93	9	3

	tens	ones
98	9	8

	tens	ones
94	9	4

	tens	ones
99	9	9

Name_____

Use the Place Value Chart

Use the place value chart to build each number. **Write** the numbers in the table.

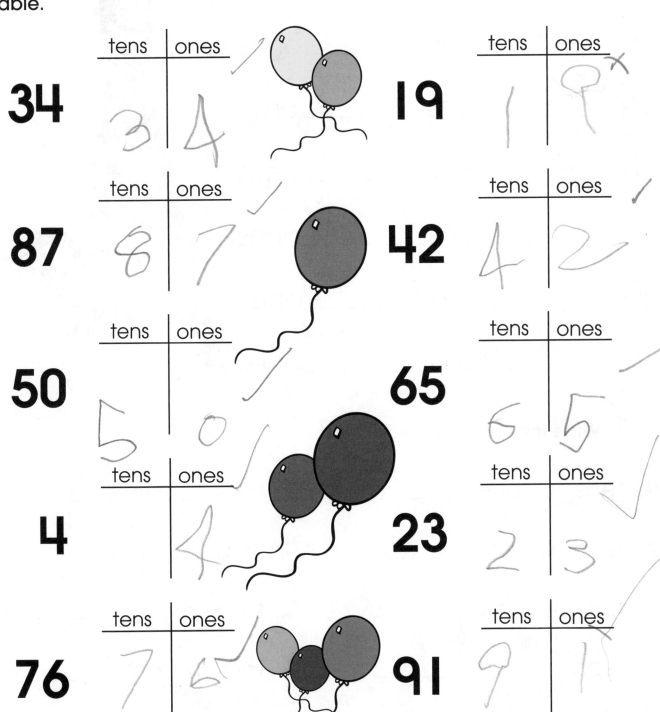

34

tens	ones
3	4

19

tens	ones
1	9

87

tens	ones
8	7

42

tens	ones
4	2

50

tens	ones
5	0

65

tens	ones
6	5

4

tens	ones
	4

23

tens	ones
2	3

76

tens	ones
7	6

91

tens	ones
9	1

Name_____

Write the Value

 Write the value of each number below.

35 _____ tens _____ ones

19 _____ tens _____ ones

8 _____ tens _____ ones

26 _____ tens _____ ones

49 _____ tens _____ ones

10 _____ tens _____ ones

 Write the numbers below.

4 tens 6 ones _____   3 tens 2 ones _____

2 tens 9 ones _____   4 tens 0 ones _____

1 ten 4 ones _____   0 tens 6 ones _____

2 tens 1 one _____   4 tens 7 ones _____

3 tens 3 ones _____   1 ten 1 one _____

Name_____

Add the Ones and the Tens

Add the ones and tens. **Write** the answer on the blank.

Example:

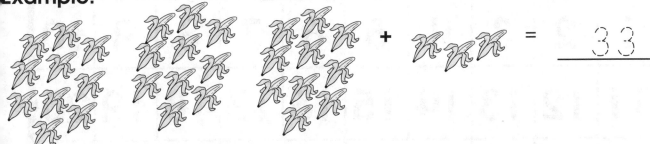

3 tens   +   **3 ones**   =   **33**___

7 tens + 5 ones = _____   4 tens + 0 ones = _____

2 tens + 3 ones = _____   8 tens + 1 one = _____

5 tens + 2 ones = _____   1 ten + 1 one = _____

5 tens + 4 ones = _____   6 tens + 3 ones = _____

9 tens + 5 ones = _____   3 tens + 7 ones = _____

Draw a line to the correct number.

6 tens + 7 ones   73

4 tens + 2 ones   67

8 tens + 0 ones   51

7 tens + 3 ones   80

5 tens + 1 one   42

Name_____

Count the Numbers

Count the numbers from **1–100**.

1	2	3	4	5	6	7	8	9	10
11	12	13	14	15	16	17	18	19	20
21	22	23	24	25	26	27	28	29	30
31	32	33	34	35	36	37	38	39	40
41	42	43	44	45	46	47	48	49	50
51	52	53	54	55	56	57	58	59	60
61	62	63	64	65	66	67	68	69	70
71	72	73	74	75	76	77	78	79	80
81	82	83	84	85	86	87	88	89	90
91	92	93	94	95	96	97	98	99	100

Name_____

Color 30–69

Color the ball **red** if the number is **30–39**.   **Color** the ball **purple** if the number is **40–49**.   **Color** the ball **blue** if the number is **50–59**.

Color the ball **green** if the number is **60–69**.

Name_____

Connect the Dots

Connect the dots in order from **1–75**. **Color** the animal.

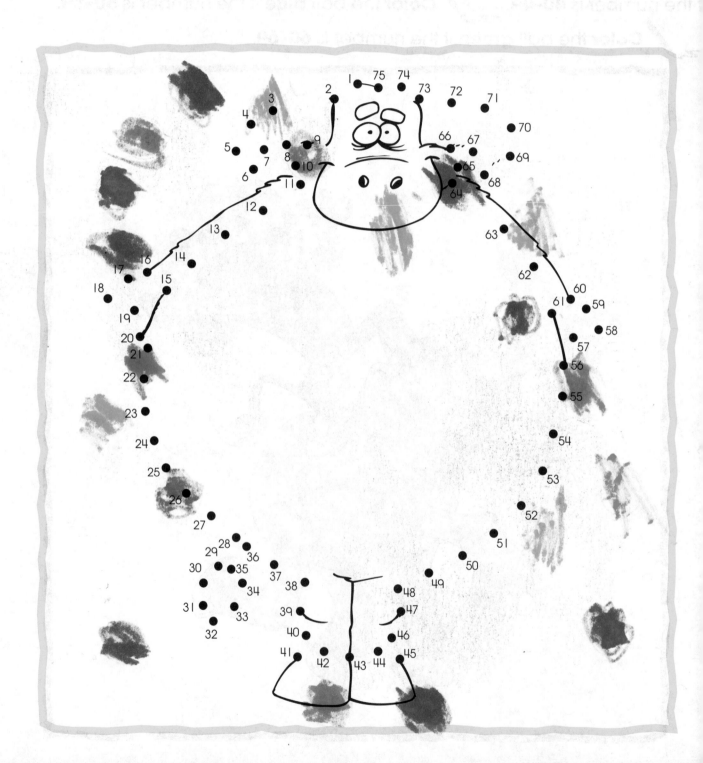

Name_____

Color the Bubbles

Color the bubble **red** if the number is **1-25**. Color the bubble **orange** if the number is **26-50**. Color the bubble **yellow** if the number is **51-75**. Color the bubble **blue** if the number is **76-100**.

Counting

Name_____

Count by 2's

This is how to count by **2's**. Begin with the number **2**. If you add **2**, you get **4**. If you add **2** more, you get **6**, and so on. Use the number line to help you.

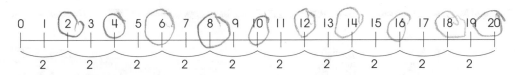

Count by **2's** to **draw** the path to the store.

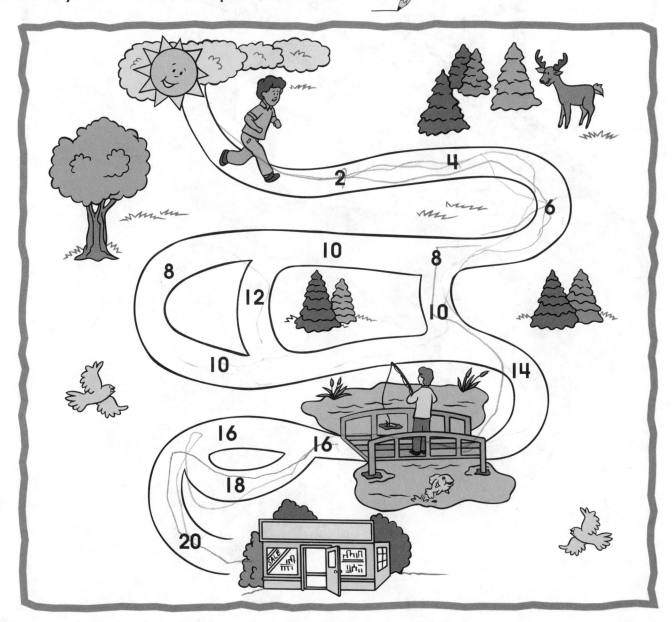

Name_____

Count by 2's

Count by **2's**. ✏️ **Write** the numbers to **30** in the water drops. Begin at the top of the slide and go down.

Count by 2's

Count by 2's. ✏️ **Write** the numbers on the notes.

Use the letters on the notes to find out the name of the song the frog is singing.

"___ ___ , ___ ___ ___ ___   ___ ___

28 22   2   2   4   22

___ ___ ___ ___ ___ ___ ___ ___

16 44 26 36 38   6   10 18

___ ___ ___ ___ ___   ___ ___ ___

44 26 40 10   8   48 32 22

___ ___ ___ ___ ___ ___ ___ ___ "

4   36 16 38 30 50 44   8

Name_____

Count by 5's

This is how to count by **5's**. Begin with the number **5**. If you add **5**, you get **10**. If you add **5** more, you get **15**, and so on. Use the number line to help you.

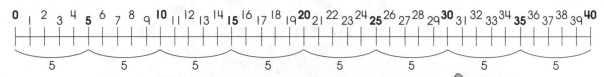

Count by **5's** to **draw** the path to the playground.

Name _____

Count by 2's and 5's

Count by **2's**. 🖉 **Trace** then **write** the numbers below.

| 2 | 4 | 6 | 8 | 10 | 12 | 14 | 16 | 20 | 22 |

Count by **5's**. 🖉 **Trace** then **write** the numbers below.

| 5 | 10 | 15 | 20 | 25 | 30 | 35 | 40 | 45 | 50 |

Count by **2's**. **Connect** the dots.

Color the picture. 🖍

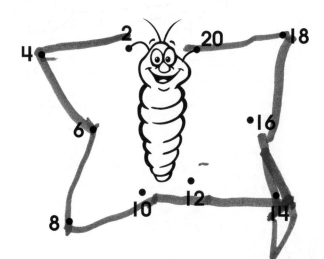

Count by **5's**. **Connect** the dots.

Color the picture. 🖍

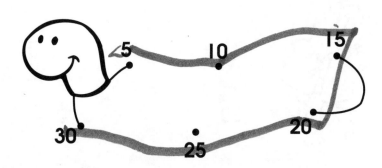

Name_____

Count by 5's

Find out what holds something good! **Count** by **5's** to connect the dots.

Color the picture.

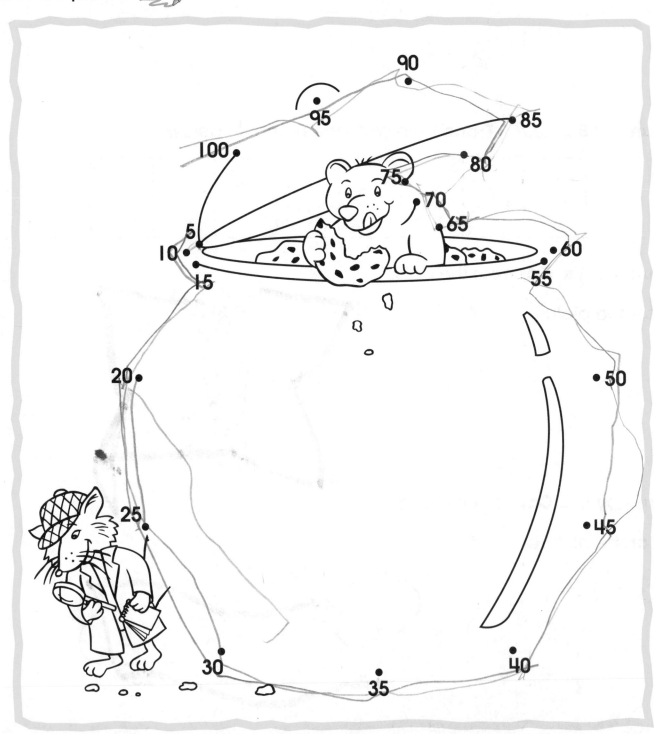

Name_____

Count by 5's

Help the bird count the twigs needed to build its nest. **Count** by **5's**.

Write the numbers in the boxes.

Name_____

Count by 10's

This is how to count by **10's**. Begin with the number **10**. If you add **10**, you get **20**. If you add **10** more, you get **30**, and so on. Use the number line to help you.

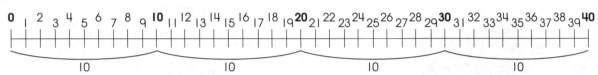

Count by **10's**. **Color** each canteen as you count by **10** to lead the camel to the watering hole.

Count by 5's and 10's

**Count by 5's.
Draw triangles
around each
number in the box.**

1	2	3	4	5	6	7	8	9	10
11	12	13	14	15	16	17	18	19	20
21	22	23	24	25	26	27	28	29	30
31	32	33	34	35	36	37	38	39	40
41	42	43	44	45	46	47	48	49	50

Count by 5's.

5   10   ___   ___   ___   ___   ___

___   ___

**Count by 10's.
Draw boxes
around each
number in the box.**

1	2	3	4	5	6	7	8	9	10
11	12	13	14	15	16	17	18	19	20
21	22	23	24	25	26	27	28	29	30
31	32	33	34	35	36	37	38	39	40
41	42	43	44	45	46	47	48	49	50

Count by 10's.

10   ___   ___   ___   ___

Name_____

Count by 10's

Count by **10's** to complete each row. ✏️ **Write** the numbers below each basket.

20   30   40   50   60

50   60   70   80   90

40   50   60   70   80

30   40   50   60   70

Name

Write the Missing Numbers

Write the missing numbers.

Count by 2's:

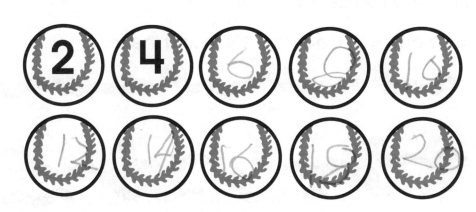

Count by 5's:

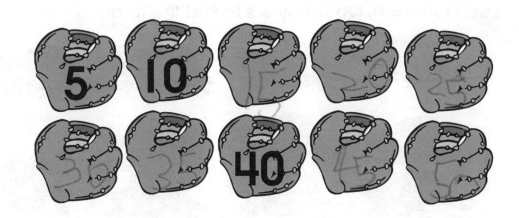

Count by 10's:

Name_____

Count by 2's, 5's, and 10's

Count by **2's**, **5's**, and **10's** to find the "critter count." ✏️ **Write** the number on the line beside each row.

Each worm = **2**. **Count** by **2's** to find the total.

= _____

= _____

Each turtle = **5**. **Count** by **5's** to find the total.

= _____

= _____

Each ladybug = **10**. **Count** by **10's** to find the total.

= _____

= _____

Name_____

First for 1, Second for 2...

Another way of counting is **first** for **1**, **second** for **2**, **third** for **3**, and so on. These are called **ordinal numbers**.

Color the **second** ball **brown**.

Color the **sixth** ball **yellow**.

Color the **fourth** ball **orange**.

Color the **first** ball **black**.

Color the **fifth** ball **green**.

Color the **seventh** ball **purple**.

1 2 3 4 5 6 7 8

Name_____

Ordinal Numbers

Next to each ordinal number, **write** the color of the car in that position.

first _____ fifth

seventh _____ tenth

third _____ sixth

fourth _____ second

eighth _____ ninth

Name_____

Write Each Word

Write each word on the correct line to put the words in order.

second	fifth	seventh	first	tenth
third	eighth	sixth	fourth	ninth

1. _____   6. _____

2. _____   7. _____

3. _____   8. _____

4. _____   9. _____

5. _____   10. _____

Which picture is circled in each row?  **Underline** the word that tells the correct number.

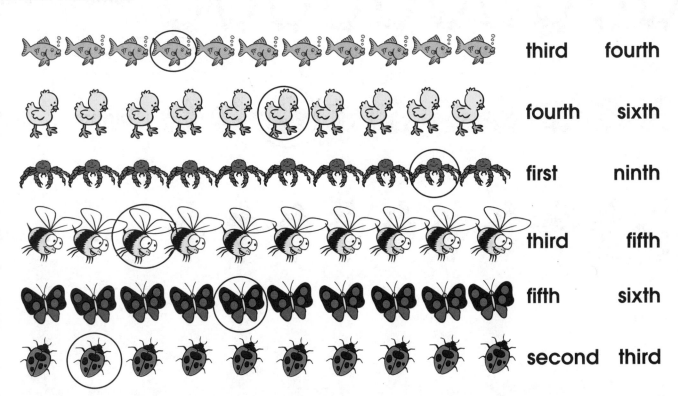

third   fourth

fourth   sixth

first   ninth

third   fifth

fifth   sixth

second   third

Name_____

Write Each Word

Which picture is circled in each row? **Underline** the word that tells the correct number.

 first   fourth

 third   seventh

 tenth   sixth

 eighth   fifth

 third   second

Comparing

Name_____

Circle the Correct Numbers

Circle the correct numbers in each box.

Numbers less than 3

| 1 | 2 | 3 | 4 | 5 | 6 | 7 | 8 | 9 | 10 | 11 | 12 |

Numbers greater than 10

| 1 | 2 | 3 | 4 | 5 | 6 | 7 | 8 | 9 | 10 | 11 | 12 |

Numbers equal to 7

| 1 | 2 | 3 | 4 | 5 | 6 | 7 | 8 | 9 | 10 | 11 | 12 |

Numbers greater than 2

| 1 | 2 | 3 | 4 | 5 | 6 | 7 | 8 | 9 | 10 | 11 | 12 |

Numbers less than 10

| 1 | 2 | 3 | 4 | 5 | 6 | 7 | 8 | 9 | 10 | 11 | 12 |

Numbers greater than 7

| 1 | 2 | 3 | 4 | 5 | 6 | 7 | 8 | 9 | 10 | 11 | 12 |

Name _____

Smallest and Largest

In each shape, **circle** the smallest number. **Draw** a square around the largest number.

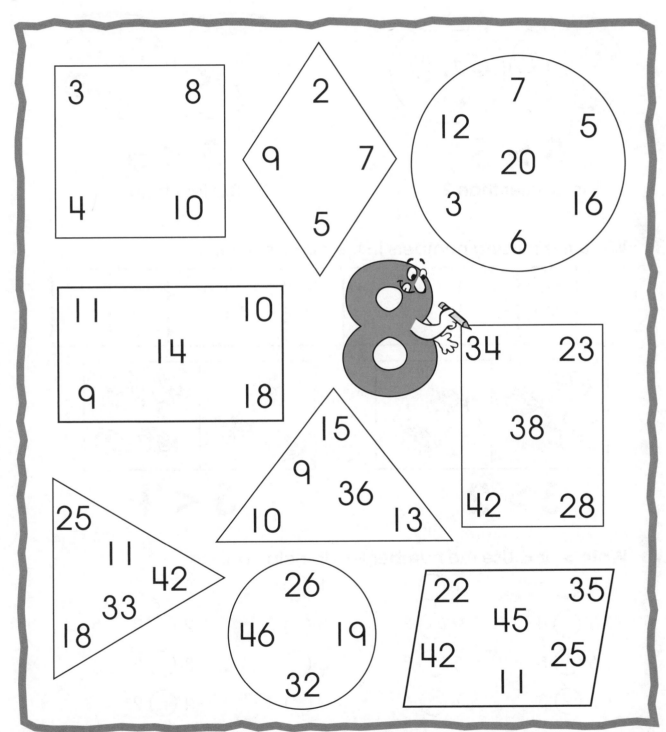

Name_____

Greater Than, Less Than

The symbol **>** means the first number is **greater than** the second number. The symbol **<** means the first number is **less than** the second number.

5 > 3

5 is greater than **3**

3 < 5

3 is less than **5**

✏️ **Write** the missing numbers in the number line.

1	2			6				

3 > 2

3 < 4

✏️ **Write > or <.** Use the number line to help you.

5 ◯ 7	1 ◯ 7	1 ◯ 9	8 ◯ 5
3 ◯ 4	9 ◯ 3	8 ◯ 7	2 ◯ 4
6 ◯ 5	5 ◯ 3	5 ◯ 7	3 ◯ 5
7 ◯ 3	7 ◯ 6	2 ◯ 8	4 ◯ 2

Name _____

Circle the Numbers

Circle the numbers in each line that make the sentence correct.

3	<	0	1	2	3	4	5	6	7	8	9	10

7	>	0	1	2	3	4	5	6	7	8	9	10

4	=	0	1	2	3	4	5	6	7	8	9	10

8	<	0	1	2	3	4	5	6	7	8	9	10

2	>	0	1	2	3	4	5	6	7	8	9	10

5	<	0	1	2	3	4	5	6	7	8	9	10

10	>	0	1	2	3	4	5	6	7	8	9	10

1	>	9	4	0

0	<	2	7	10

9	=	4	8	9

Name_____

Write < or >

✏ **Write < or >** in each circle. Make sure the "mouth" is open toward the greater number.

36 ⟨<⟩ 49   35 ⟨<⟩ 53

20 ⟨>⟩ 18   74 ⟨>⟩ 21

53 ⟨<⟩ 76   68 ⟨<⟩ 80

29 ⟨>⟩ 26   45 ⟨>⟩ 19

90 ⟨>⟩ 89   70 ⟨>⟩ 67

Compare the Numbers

Compare the numbers. **Write** the answer to each question on the line.

Which is **greater**? __58__

How much **greater**? __3__

Which is **greater**? __75__

How much **greater**? __3__

Which is **less**? __87__

How much **less**? _____

Which is **less**? __110__

How much **less**? __7__

Which is **greater**? _____

How much **greater**? _____

Name_____

Who has the Most?

Who has the **most**?   **Circle** the correct answer.

1. Traci has **3** 🐞s.

   Bob has **4** 🐞s.

   Bill has **5** 🐞s.

   Who has the **most** 🐞s?

   Traci Bob Bill

2. Pam has **7** 🐶s.

   Joe has **5** 🐶s.

   Jane has **6** 🐶s.

   Who has the **most** 🐶s?

   Pam Joe Jane

3. Jennifer has **23** 🐂s.

   Sandy has **19** 🐂s.

   Jack has **25** 🐂s.

   Who has the **most** 🐂s?

   Jennifer Sandy Jack

4. Ali has **19** 🐛s.

   Burt has **18** 🐛s.

   Brent has **17** 🐛s.

   Who has the **most** 🐛s?

   Ali Burt Brent

5. The boys have **14** 🐱s.

   The girls have **16** 🐱s.

   The teachers have **17** 🐱s.

   Who has the **most** 🐱s?

   boys girls teachers

6. Rose has **12** 🐰s.

   Betsy has **11** 🐰s.

   Leslie has **13** 🐰s.

   Who has the **most** 🐰s?

   Rose Betsy Leslie

Who has the Fewest?

Who has the **fewest**? **Circle** the correct answer.

1. Pat had **4** s.

   Charles had **3** s.

   Andrea had **5** s.

   Who had the **fewest** number

   of s?

       Pat   Charles   Andrea

2. Jeff has **5** s.

   John has **4** s.

   Bill has **6** s.

   Who has the **fewest** number

   of s?

       Jeff   John   Bill

3. Jane has **7** s.

   Susan has **9** s.

   Fred has **8** s.

   Who has the **fewest** number

   of s?

       Jane   Susan   Fred

4. Charles bought **12** s.

   Rose bought **6** s.

   Dawn bought **24** s.

   Who bought the **fewest** number

   of s?

       Charles   Rose   Dawn

5. John had **9** 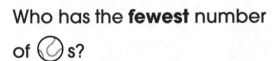s.

   Jack had **8** 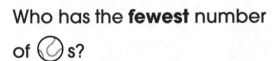s.

   Mark had **7** 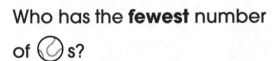s.

   Who had the **fewest** number

   of s?

       John   Jack   Mark

6. Edith bought **12** s.

   Michelle bought **16** s.

   Marty bought **13** s.

   Who bought the **fewest** number

   of s?

       Edith   Michelle   Marty

Addition
and Subtraction

Name_____

Count the Number

Count the number in each group and **write** the number on the line.

Then, **add** the groups together and **write** the sum.

 _8_ strawberries

_5_ strawberries

How many in all? _13_

 _5_ cookies

_6_ cookies

How many in all? _11_

 _7_ shoes

 _6_ shoes

How many in all? _13_

 _3_ balloons

 _9_ balloons

How many in all? _12_

 _8_ balls

 _3_ balls

How many in all? _11_

 _7_ flowers

 _2_ flowers

How many in all? _14_

Name_____

Addition Sentences

Look at the pictures. Write the answer to each addition sentence. The first one is done for you.

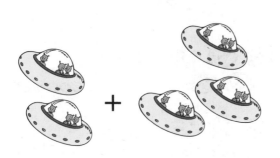

2 + 3 = __5__

1 + 7 = __8__

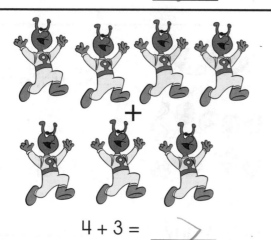

4 + 3 = __7__

5 + 0 = __5__

3 + 3 = __6__

4 + 5 = __9__

Addition Sentences

Look at the pictures. Complete the addition sentence. Write your answer in the doghouse.

2 + 6 =

7 + 3 =

6 + 1 =

4 + 5 = 9

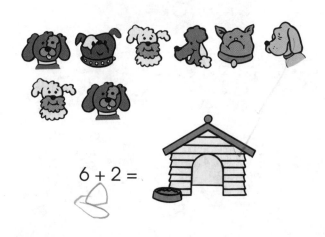

6 + 2 =

7 + 2 =

Name_____

Addition Sentences

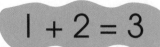 **Circle** the picture that matches the addition sentence.

1 + 2 = 3	3 + 2 = 5
2 + 4 = 6	3 + 3 = 6
3 + 4 = 7	1 + 6 = 7

Name _____

Addition Sentences

Draw the missing pictures. Write the answer to each addition sentence.

_____ + 2 = 3

_____ + 3 = 6

_____ + 0 =

5 + _2_ = 7

_____ + 3 = 5

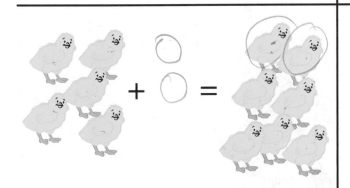

_____ + 4 = 8

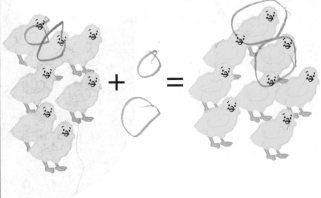

7 + _2_ = 8

Name_____

Add to Find the Sum

Add to find each sum.

$$\begin{array}{r} 4 \\ +3 \\ \hline 7 \end{array}$$

$$\begin{array}{r} 0 \\ +6 \\ \hline 6 \end{array}$$

$$\begin{array}{r} 2 \\ +4 \\ \hline 6 \end{array}$$

$$\begin{array}{r} 0 \\ +7 \\ \hline 7 \end{array}$$

$$\begin{array}{r} 1 \\ +6 \\ \hline 7 \end{array}$$

$$\begin{array}{r} 3 \\ +4 \\ \hline 7 \end{array}$$

$$\begin{array}{r} 6 \\ +0 \\ \hline 6 \end{array}$$

$$\begin{array}{r} 1 \\ +5 \\ \hline 6 \end{array}$$

$$\begin{array}{r} 2 \\ +5 \\ \hline 7 \end{array}$$

If the sum is **6**, color the area **blue**.

If the sum is **7**, color the area yellow.

Name_____

Add to Find the Sum

Add to find each sum. Use the code to **color** the picture.

1 – white	2 – yellow	3 – orange	4 – purple	5 – red
6 – pink	7 – gray	8 – brown	9 – green	10 – blue

Name_____

Add to Find the Sum

Add to find each sum. **Connect** the dots in order. Use the sums and the letters from the boxes to answer the riddle.

G 5 + 3	A 6 + 6	T 2 + 2	W 7 + 6	C 3 + 2
L 8 + 8	R 7 + 8	Y 5 + 5	U 4 + 3	E 9 + 9
N 2 + 9	O 5 + 4	P 9 + 8	I 6 + 8	E 1 + 2

Riddle: What do you get when you cross an eel and a goat?

$$\overline{10}\ \overline{9}\ \overline{7}\ \ \ \overline{13}\ \overline{14}\ \overline{16}\ \overline{16}$$

$$\overline{8}\ \overline{18}\ \overline{4}\ \ \ \overline{12}\ \overline{11}$$

$$\overline{3}\ \overline{16}\ \overline{18}\ \overline{5}\ \overline{4}\ \overline{15}\ \overline{14}\ \overline{5}$$

$$\overline{5}\ \overline{12}\ \overline{11}$$

$$\overline{9}\ \overline{17}\ \overline{18}\ \overline{11}\ \overline{18}\ \overline{15}$$

PEARS

Name _____

Count the Objects

Count the objects and fill in the blanks. Then, switch the numbers and **write** another addition sentence. The first one is done for you.

Example:

If ___3___ + ___8___ = ___11___ , so does ___8___ + ___3___ .

If ___8___ + ___9___ = ___17___ , so does ___9___ + ___8___ .

If ___7___ + ___8___ = ___15___ , so does ___8___ + ___7___ .

If ___4___ + ___6___ = ___10___ , so does ___6___ + ___4___ .

If ___6___ + ___7___ = ___13___ , so does ___7___ + ___6___ .

Name_____

Adding 3 Numbers

When adding three numbers, **add** two numbers first, then **add** the third to that sum. To decide which two numbers to add first, try one of these strategies.

Look for doubles.

```
  8            4            2
  3  >6        4 >8         9 >4
+ 3          + 5          + 2
────         ────         ────
 14           13           13
```

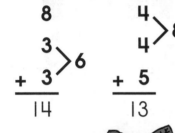

Look for a 10.

```
  7            8            1
  3 >10        4            5 >10
+ 4          + 6 >10      + 9
────         ────         ────
 14           18           15
```

Add to find the sum of these numbers. Look for a **10** or **doubles**.

```
   5            2            7            3            6
   5            6            1            7            2
 + 4          + 8          + 7          + 4          + 6
─────        ─────        ─────        ─────        ─────


   7            7            6            5
   6            8            7            5
 + 6          + 3          + 4          + 3
─────        ─────        ─────        ─────
```

Name_____

Add to Find the Sum

Add to find the sum. If the sum is 11 or more, **color** the cone **brown**.

If the sum is less than 11, **color** the cone **yellow**.

Riddle

Solve each row from left to right. ✏️ **Write** the letters on the lines below to answer the riddle. **Connect** the dots in the order of the answers.

E	3	H	2	S	4	Y	7	A	4	O	7
	4		9		4		9		5		7
+	7	+	1	+	7	+	3	+	8	+	2

B	9	P	8	T	9	I	5	V	6	R	9
	8		4		9		2		2		6
+	5	+	6	+	6	+	1	+	3	+	6

What do a race car and a zebra have in common?

____ ____ ____ ____   ____ ____ ____ ____
22   16   24   12   12   17   11   14

____ ____ ____ ____ ____ ____ ____
15   24   21   8   18   14   15

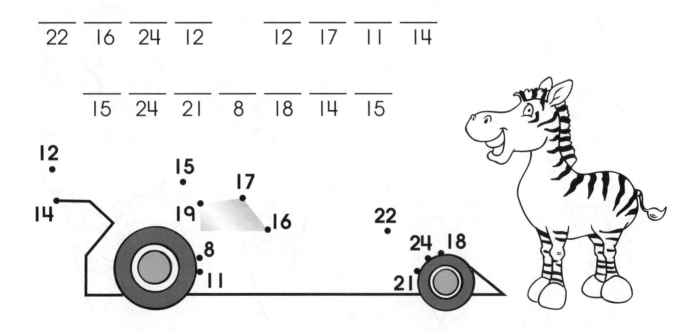

Add to Find the Sum

Add to find the sums.   **Write** the letters on the lines.

What do you call a mummy who eats crackers in bed?

| 15 | 14 | 12 | 16 | 9 | 17 | 7 | 11 | 18 | 13 | 8 | 10 |

M	M	A
7 + 3 + 1 =	7 + 0 + 2 =	6 + 4 + 5 =
C	**Y**	**M**
5 + 6 + 3 =	2 + 2 + 6 =	5 + 3 + 5 =
M	**R**	**Y**
8 + 2 + 7 =	5 + 4 + 3 =	4 + 2 + 1 =
U	**M**	**U**
8 + 3 + 5 =	6 + 2 + 0 =	8 + 1 + 9 =

Name_____

Count Back

Use the number line to **count back**.

Example: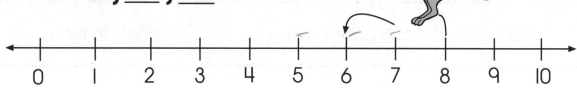

8, _7_ , _6_

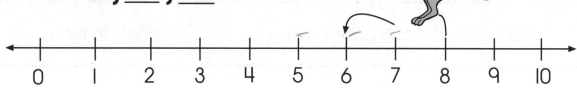

0 1 2 3 4 5 6 7 8 9 10

Write your answer on the line.

7 - 3 = _4_

7, __, __, __

6 - 2 = _4_

6, __, __

8 - 1 = _7_

8, __

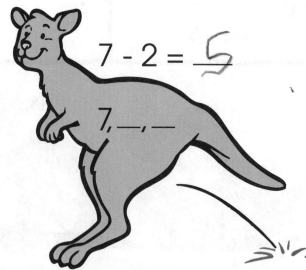

7 - 2 = _5_

7, __, __

Name _____

Subtraction Sentences

Look at the pictures. **Write** the answer to each subtraction sentence.

4 - 1 = __3__

6 - 2 = __4__

5 - 3 = __2__

7 - 3 = __4__

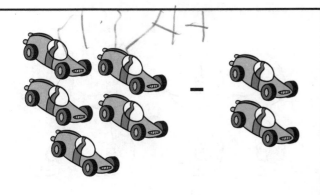

5 - 2 = __3__

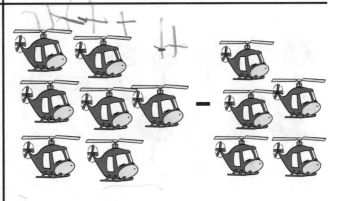

7 - 5 = __2__

Name_____

Subtraction Sentences

Look at the pictures. **Write** the answer to each subtraction sentence.

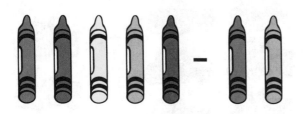

5 - 2 = __3__

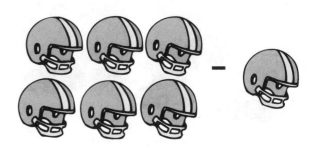

6 - 1 = __5__

7 - 4 = __3__

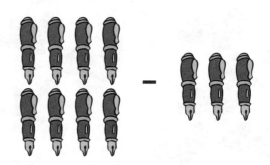

8 - 3 = __5__

9 - 2 = __7__

4 - 4 = __0__

Name_____

Subtraction Sentences

Solve the subtraction sentences below. ✏️ **Write** each answer on a rubber duck.

Name _____

Difference

Color the two numbers in each box that show the given difference.

Difference of 1

6	4
3	8

3	1
5	6

4	0
1	7

Difference of 1

3	7
1	8

2	3
5	7

6	3
9	7

Difference of 2

3	0
7	1

3	8
6	9

7	1
4	5

Difference of 2

3	4
8	2

7	4
10	5

10	8
5	4

Difference of 0

2	1
4	2

7	3
8	3

5	6
5	4

Name_____

Difference

Circle the two numbers next to each other that make the given difference. Find as many as you can in each row.

Difference of 1

2 3 0 8 7 2 9 10 6 5 1 4 4 3

Difference of 1

8 4 5 3 7 1 2 4 9 8 0 1 7 6

Difference of 2

5 4 2 3 1 0 2 5 8 9 7 6 8 5

Difference of 2

7 5 10 8 1 4 6 3 1 6 7 9 2 0

Difference of 3

1 6 3 2 8 4 7 6 10 7 3 9 5 2

Wrong Answer

Draw an **X** on the nose of each worm with the wrong answer. Find 6 wrong answers.

Name_____

Subtraction Sentences

Solve the subtraction sentences below. Use the code to **color** the picture.

0 – green	**2** – blue	**4** – black
1 – brown	**3** – purple	**5** – pink

Name_____

Count the Candy

Count the candy in each dish. 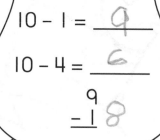 **Write** the number on the line by each dish.  **Circle** each problem with the same answer.

$7 - 1 =$ __6__

$\begin{array}{r} 8 \\ -2 \\ \hline 6 \end{array}$

_____

$10 - 1 =$ __9__

$10 - 4 =$ __6__

$\begin{array}{r} 9 \\ -1 \\ \hline 8 \end{array}$

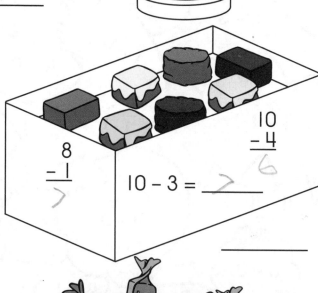

$\begin{array}{r} 8 \\ -1 \\ \hline 7 \end{array}$

$10 - 3 =$ __7__

$\begin{array}{r} 10 \\ -4 \\ \hline 6 \end{array}$

_____

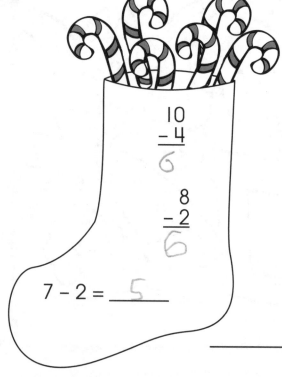

$\begin{array}{r} 10 \\ -4 \\ \hline 6 \end{array}$

$\begin{array}{r} 8 \\ -2 \\ \hline 6 \end{array}$

$7 - 2 =$ __5__

_____

$\begin{array}{r} 9 \\ -4 \\ \hline 5 \end{array}$

$\begin{array}{r} 9 \\ -1 \\ \hline 8 \end{array}$

$7 - 2 =$ __5__

_____

Name_____

Secret Message

Write the answers to the subtraction problems. Use the code to find the secret message.

Code:

7	5	2	6	4	3
K	T	Y	E	W	A

PLEASE, DON'T EVER

8 -3	10 - 7	9 -2	10 - 4
5	3	>	6

___	___	___	___

9 -6	6 -2	7 -4	8 -6
3	4	3	2

___	___	___	___

MY MATH!

5 – 6

Subtraction Sentences

Solve the subtraction sentences below. Use the code to **color** the picture.

1 – **white**	2 – **purple**	3 – **black**	4 – **green**	5 – **yellow**
6 – **blue**	7 – **pink**	8 – **gray**	9 – **orange**	10 – **red**

Subtract

Subtract to find the difference.

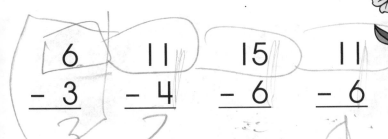

6	11	15	11
− 3	− 4	− 6	− 6

12	10	12	10	13	8	12
− 3	− 6	− 4	− 5	− 5	− 7	− 3

14	17	11	15	14	10	13
− 8	− 9	− 8	− 7	− 9	− 3	− 4

9	12	14	8	12	18	14
− 6	− 9	− 6	− 5	− 7	− 9	− 6

8	12	18	14	13	13	17
− 5	− 7	− 9	− 6	− 8	− 6	− 8

Name _____

+ or –

Look at the pictures. *Write* + or – in the circles. **Write** the answers to the number sentences.

$5 \oplus 6 = 11$

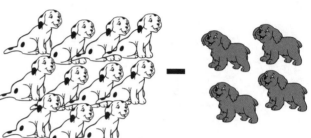

$11 \bigcirc 4 = \underline{\quad}$

$12 \bigcirc 7 = \underline{\quad}$

$7 \oplus 6 = 13$

$5 \otimes 5 = 10$

$8 \oplus 6 = 14$

Name_____

+ or -

✏️ **Write** + or – in the magnifying glass to make each problem correct.

Circle the four problems that will not work with either sign.

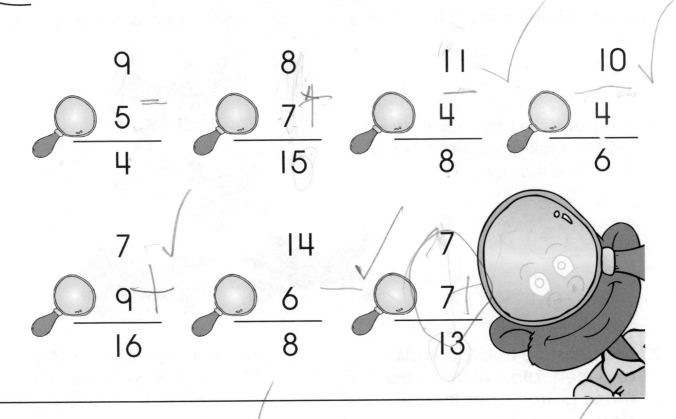

$$\begin{array}{r} 9 \\ 5 \\ \hline 4 \end{array}$$

$$\begin{array}{r} 8 \\ 7 \\ \hline 15 \end{array}$$

$$\begin{array}{r} 11 \\ 4 \\ \hline 8 \end{array}$$

$$\begin{array}{r} 10 \\ 4 \\ \hline 6 \end{array}$$

$$\begin{array}{r} 7 \\ 9 \\ \hline 16 \end{array}$$

$$\begin{array}{r} 14 \\ 6 \\ \hline 8 \end{array}$$

$$\begin{array}{r} 7 \\ 7 \\ \hline 13 \end{array}$$

6 ⊕ 7 = 13

13 ⊖ 9 = 4

15 ⊖ 9 = 6

9 ⊕ 2 = 12

10 ⊖ 3 = 6

8 ⊕ 8 = 16

bonus

+ or –

Should you add or subtract? The key words "in all" tell you to add. The key word "left" tells you to subtract. **Circle** the key words and **write + or –** in the circles. Then, solve the problems. The first one is done for you.

1. The pet store has 3 large dogs and 5 small dogs. How many dogs are there (in all)?

$$3 \; \oplus \; 5 = \underline{\textbf{8}}$$

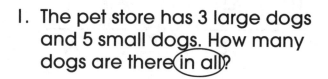

2. The pet store had 9 parrots and then sold 4 of them. How many parrots does the pet store have left?

$$9 \; \bigcirc \; 4 = \underline{\quad}$$

4. The pet store gave Linda's class 2 adult gerbils and 9 young ones. How many gerbils did Linda's class get in all?

$$2 \; \bigcirc \; 9 = \underline{\quad}$$

3. At the pet store, 3 of the 8 kittens were sold. How many kittens are left in the pet store?

$$8 \; \bigcirc \; 3 = \underline{\quad}$$

5. The monkey at the pet store has 5 rubber toys and 4 wooden toys. How many toys does the monkey have in all?

$$5 \; \bigcirc \; 4 = \underline{\quad}$$

Name_____

+ or –

Write the answer to the number problem under each picture. **Write +** or – to show if you should add or subtract.

4   +   5

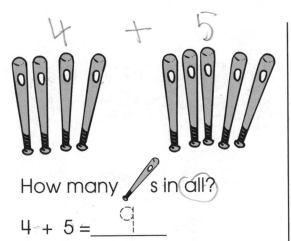

How many s in all?

4 + 5 = ___9___

How many s in all?

7 + 5 = ___12___

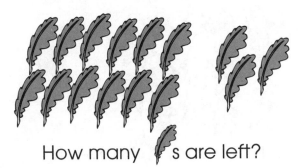

How many s are left?

12   3 = _____

How many s are left?

15   8 = _____

How many s in all?

5 + 8 = ___13___

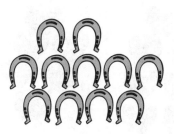

How many s are left?

11   4 = _____

Name_____

+ or -

✏ **Write** the answer to the number problem under each picture. **Write +** or **–** to show if you should add or subtract.

How many  in all?

7 + 5 = __12__

How many 🧀s in all?

8 ✗ 3 = __11__

How many 🌸s are left?

9 ─ 4 = __5__

How many 🍪s are left?

14 ─ 1 = __13__

How many 🦋s in all?

15 ┼ 6 = __21__

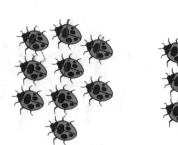

How many 🐞s are left?

9 ─ 5 = __4__

Name_____

Solve the Problems

Draw a line under the question that matches the picture. Then, solve the problems.

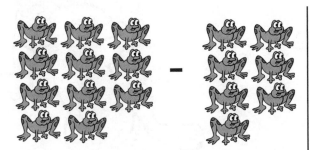

How many 🐸s are there in all?
How many 🐸s are left?

11 – 7 = ____4____

How many 🐙s are there in all?
How many 🐙s are left?

4 + 5 = _____

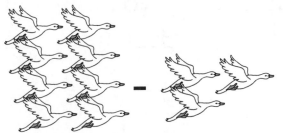

How many 🦆s are there in all?
How many 🦆s are left?

8 – 3 = _____

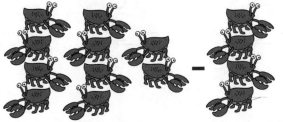

How many 🦀s are there in all?
How many 🦀s are left?

10 – 4 = _____

How many 🐊s are there in all?
How many 🐊s are left?

5 + 6 = _____

How many 🕊s are there in all?
How many 🕊s are left?

8 + 4 = _____

Name_____

Add or Subtract

Add or **subtract** to solve each problem.  **Circle** the answers that are less than 10.

Example:

$$\begin{array}{r} 3 \\ +1 \\ \hline 4 \end{array}$$ ④

$$\begin{array}{r} 3 \\ -1 \\ \hline 2 \end{array}$$ ②

$$\begin{array}{r} 9 \\ +3 \\ \hline 12 \end{array}$$

$$\begin{array}{r} 6 \\ -2 \\ \hline \end{array}$$

$$\begin{array}{r} 12 \\ -1 \\ \hline \end{array}$$

$$\begin{array}{r} 18 \\ +1 \\ \hline 19 \end{array}$$

$$\begin{array}{r} 15 \\ -6 \\ \hline \end{array}$$

$$\begin{array}{r} 7 \\ +6 \\ \hline 13 \end{array}$$

$$\begin{array}{r} 16 \\ -9 \\ \hline \end{array}$$

$$\begin{array}{r} 10 \\ -3 \\ \hline \end{array}$$

$$\begin{array}{r} 14 \\ +5 \\ \hline 19 \end{array}$$

$$\begin{array}{r} 16 \\ -8 \\ \hline \end{array}$$

$$\begin{array}{r} 8 \\ +7 \\ \hline 15 \end{array}$$

$$\begin{array}{r} 12 \\ +2 \\ \hline 14 \end{array}$$

$$\begin{array}{r} 13 \\ -4 \\ \hline \end{array}$$

$$\begin{array}{r} 17 \\ +2 \\ \hline 19 \end{array}$$

$$\begin{array}{r} 9 \\ +9 \\ \hline 18 \end{array}$$

Name_____

Add or Subtract

Add or **subtract** to solve each problem. Use the code to color the fruit.

3 – yellow   **5** – orange   **7** – yellow   **9** – red
4 – red   **6** – purple   **8** – green   **10** – brown

$$\begin{array}{r} 9 \\ -\ 4 \\ \hline 5 \end{array}$$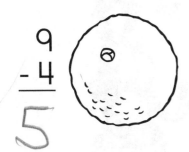

$$\begin{array}{r} 3 \\ +\ 7 \\ \hline \end{array}$$ 10

$$\begin{array}{r} 6 \\ -\ 3 \\ \hline \end{array}$$

$$\begin{array}{r} 1 \\ +\ 3 \\ \hline \end{array}$$

$$\begin{array}{r} 9 \\ -\ 2 \\ \hline 7 \end{array}$$

$$\begin{array}{r} 7 \\ +\ 2 \\ \hline \end{array}$$ 9

$$\begin{array}{r} 9 \\ -\ 1 \\ \hline \end{array}$$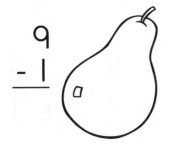

$$\begin{array}{r} 6 \\ +\ 3 \\ \hline \end{array}$$ w

$$\begin{array}{r} 8 \\ -\ 2 \\ \hline 5 \end{array}$$

Add or Subtract

Write the answers to the addition and subtraction problems below.

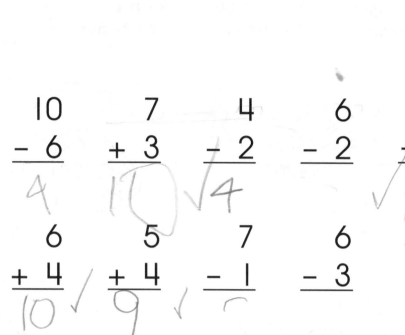

10	7	4	6	4
− 6	+ 3	− 2	− 2	+ 1

6	5	7	6
+ 4	+ 4	− 1	− 3

4	1	2	8	2	10	9
+ 3	+ 9	− 1	− 6	+ 1	− 3	− 4

3	2	6	5	5	8	5
+ 5	+ 8	− 3	+ 5	− 3	+ 2	− 4

10	5	5	9	2	3	8
− 8	− 1	+ 2	+ 2	+ 6	+ 7	+ 1

Two-Digit Addition and Subtraction

Add

Look at the examples. Follow the steps to **add**.

Examples:

$$33 \atop \underline{+41}$$ $$42 \atop \underline{+24}$$

Step 1: Add the ones.

tens	ones
3	3
+4	1
	4

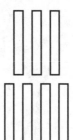 

Step 2: Add the tens.

tens	ones
3	3
+4	1
7	4

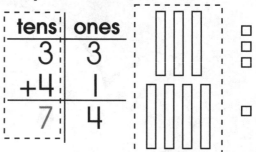

Step 1: Add the ones.

tens	ones
4	2
+2	4
	6

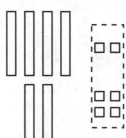

Step 2: Add the tens.

tens	ones
4	2
+2	4
6	6

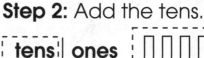

$$33 \atop \underline{+41}$$ $$15 \atop \underline{+23}$$ $$38 \atop \underline{+61}$$ $$11 \atop \underline{+26}$$ $$37 \atop \underline{+42}$$ $$72 \atop \underline{+11}$$

$$25 \atop \underline{+42}$$ $$62 \atop \underline{+14}$$ $$32 \atop \underline{+44}$$ $$25 \atop \underline{+13}$$ $$82 \atop \underline{+\ 6}$$ $$91 \atop \underline{+\ 5}$$

Add

Add the ones and then the tens in each problem.  Then, **write** the sum in the blank.

Example:

2 tens and 6 ones
+ 1 ten and 3 ones
_____

3 tens and 9 ones = 39

1 ten and 4 ones
+ 3 tens and 3 ones
_____

__ tens and __ ones = ___

2 tens and 5 ones
+ 2 tens and 3 ones
_____

__ tens and __ones = ___

1 ten and 6 ones
+ 5 tens and 1 one
_____

__ tens and __ones = ___

1 ten and 3 ones
+ 1 ten and 1 one
_____

__ tens and __ones = ___

2 tens and 5 ones
+ 2 tens and 0 ones
_____

__ tens and __ones = ___

1 ten and 5 ones
+ 2 tens and 4 ones
_____

__ tens and __ ones = ___

7 tens and 6 ones
+ 2 tens and 2 ones
_____

__ tens and __ ones = ___

Add

Add to solve the problems. **Add** the ones first. Then, **add** the tens.

tens	ones
2	5
+1	4

tens	ones
5	3
+3	2

tens	ones
7	1
+2	8

tens	ones
4	4
+3	2

tens	ones
5	1
+3	7

tens	ones
2	6
+5	2

tens	ones
2	6
+4	2

tens	ones
3	7
+5	1

tens	ones
1	9
+3	0

Add

Add the total points scored in each game. Remember to **add** the ones first, then the tens.

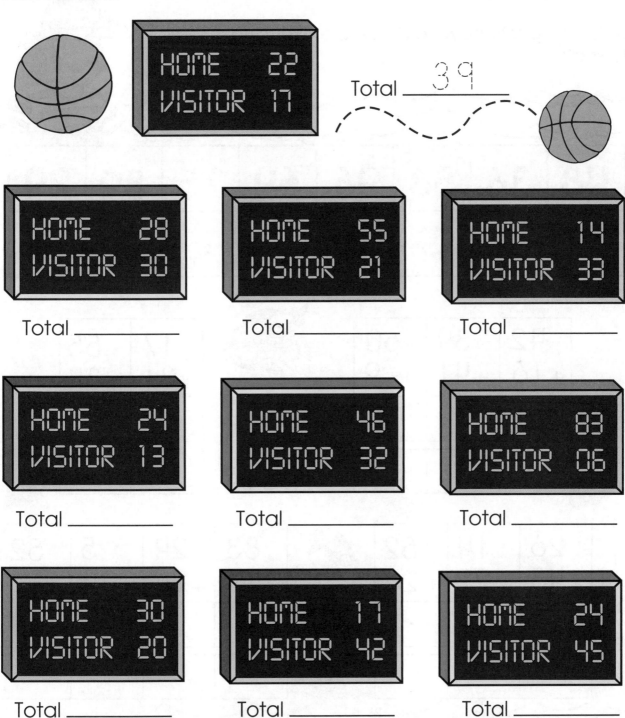

HOME 22
VISITOR 17

Total ___39___

HOME 28
VISITOR 30

Total _____

HOME 55
VISITOR 21

Total _____

HOME 14
VISITOR 33

Total _____

HOME 24
VISITOR 13

Total _____

HOME 46
VISITOR 32

Total _____

HOME 83
VISITOR 06

Total _____

HOME 30
VISITOR 20

Total _____

HOME 17
VISITOR 42

Total _____

HOME 24
VISITOR 45

Total _____

Addition Riddle

Write the answers to the addition problems. Use the code to find the answer to this riddle:

What did the pirate have to do before every trip out to sea?

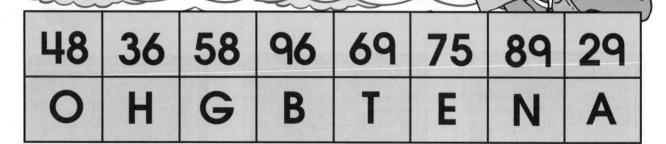

48	36	58	96	69	75	89	29
O	H	G	B	T	E	N	A

42 +16	34 +41	60 + 9
58		
G		

17 +31	55 +34

26 +43	14 +22	52 +23

83 +13	24 +24	5 +24	52 +17
			!

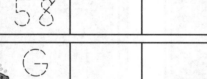

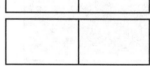

Addition Riddle

Write the answers to each problem to find the number of bees in each hive. Use the letters to solve the riddle.

K
26
+13

M
82
+15

L
12
+32

E
34
+45

J
92
+ 6

R
46
+31

B
61
+22

A
56
+12

C
70
+15

The honey was too hard to get so Ted E. Bear ate something else. What was it?

"_____ _____ _____ _____ _____"
   83   44   68   85   39

"_____ _____ _____ _____ _____   _____ _____ _____
   83   79   68   77   79   98   68   97

Subtract

Look at the example. Follow the steps to **subtract**.

Examples: $\begin{array}{r} 28 \\ -14 \\ \hline \end{array}$ $\begin{array}{r} 24 \\ -12 \\ \hline \end{array}$

Step 1: Subtract the ones.

tens	ones
2	8
-1	4
	4

Step 2: Subtract the tens.

tens	ones
2	8
-1	4
1	4

Step 1: Subtract the ones.

tens	ones
2	4
-1	2
	2

Step 2: Subtract the tens.

tens	ones
2	4
-1	2
1	2

$\begin{array}{r} 24 \\ -12 \\ \hline \end{array}$ $\begin{array}{r} 61 \\ -30 \\ \hline \end{array}$ $\begin{array}{r} 77 \\ -44 \\ \hline \end{array}$ $\begin{array}{r} 85 \\ -24 \\ \hline \end{array}$ $\begin{array}{r} 57 \\ -23 \\ \hline \end{array}$ $\begin{array}{r} 87 \\ -33 \\ \hline \end{array}$

Name_____

Subtract

Count the tens and the ones and **write** the numbers. Then, **subtract** to solve the problems.

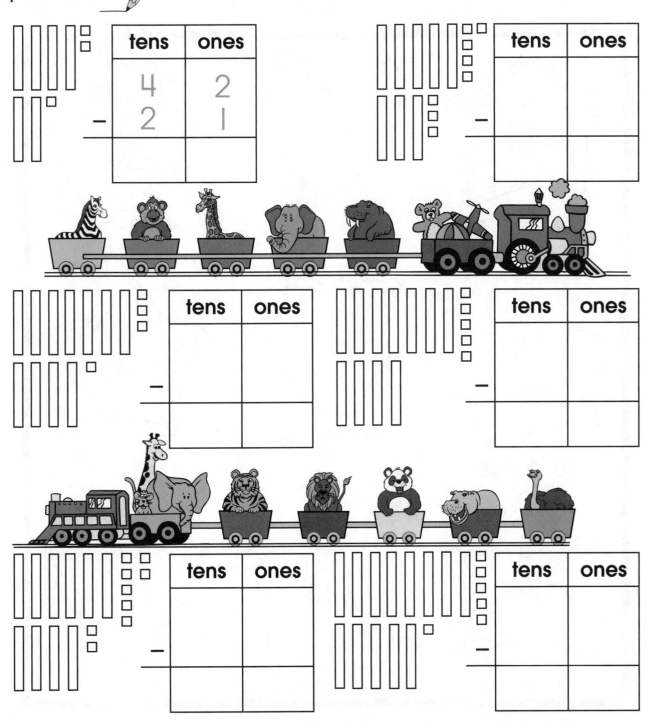

tens	ones
4	2
2	1

tens	ones

tens	ones

tens	ones

tens	ones

tens	ones

Subtract

Subtract to solve the problems.   **Circle** the answers. **Color** the cookies with answers greater than 30.

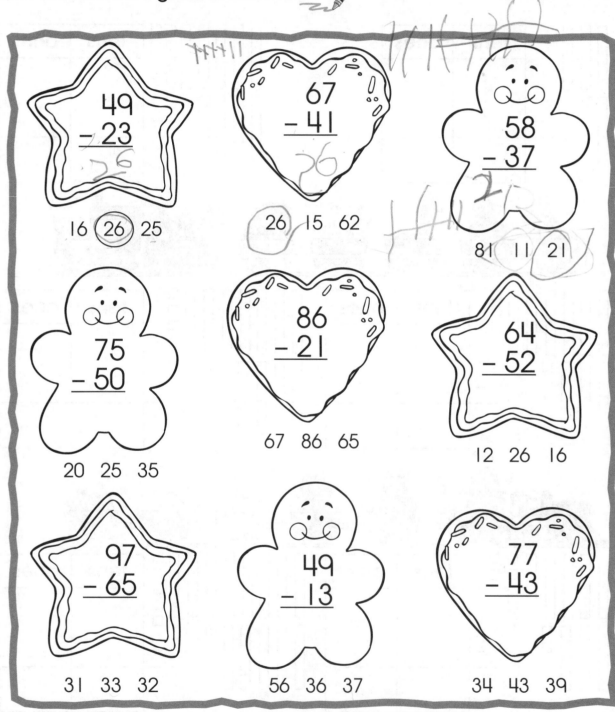

49
− 23

16   (26)   25

67
− 41

26   15   62

58
− 37

81   11   21

75
− 50

20   25   35

86
− 21

67   86   65

64
− 52

12   26   16

97
− 65

31   33   32

49
− 13

56   36   37

77
− 43

34   43   39

Subtract

Write the answers to the subtraction problems.

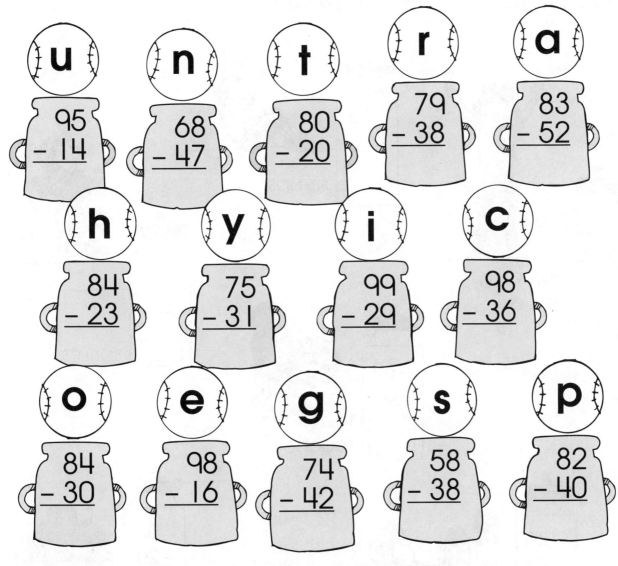

$$u \quad \begin{array}{r} 95 \\ -14 \\ \hline \end{array}$$

$$n \quad \begin{array}{r} 68 \\ -47 \\ \hline \end{array}$$

$$t \quad \begin{array}{r} 80 \\ -20 \\ \hline \end{array}$$

$$r \quad \begin{array}{r} 79 \\ -38 \\ \hline \end{array}$$

$$a \quad \begin{array}{r} 83 \\ -52 \\ \hline \end{array}$$

$$h \quad \begin{array}{r} 84 \\ -23 \\ \hline \end{array}$$

$$y \quad \begin{array}{r} 75 \\ -31 \\ \hline \end{array}$$

$$i \quad \begin{array}{r} 99 \\ -29 \\ \hline \end{array}$$

$$c \quad \begin{array}{r} 98 \\ -36 \\ \hline \end{array}$$

$$o \quad \begin{array}{r} 84 \\ -30 \\ \hline \end{array}$$

$$e \quad \begin{array}{r} 98 \\ -16 \\ \hline \end{array}$$

$$g \quad \begin{array}{r} 74 \\ -42 \\ \hline \end{array}$$

$$s \quad \begin{array}{r} 58 \\ -38 \\ \hline \end{array}$$

$$p \quad \begin{array}{r} 82 \\ -40 \\ \hline \end{array}$$

Use the answers and the letters on the baseballs to **solve** the code.

$$\overline{44} \ \overline{54} \ \overline{81} \ \overline{41} \quad \overline{42} \ \overline{70} \ \overline{60} \ \overline{62} \ \overline{61} \quad \overline{70} \ \overline{20}$$

$$\text{!}$$

$$\overline{41} \ \overline{70} \ \overline{32} \ \overline{61} \ \overline{60} \quad \overline{54} \ \overline{21} \quad \overline{60} \ \overline{31} \ \overline{41} \ \overline{32} \ \overline{82} \quad \overline{60}$$

Subtract

The players warm up before each game. **Subtract** to find out how many of each exercise the coach wants the players to do.

50
− 20

jumping
jacks

38
− 13

sit-ups

69
− 33

toe
touches

17
− 7

sprints

89
− 74

crunches

92
− 20

push-ups

What is your favorite exercise? _____

How many of them can you do? _____

Subtract

Leon the Lion was very hungry.

✏ **Write** the answers to the problems to find out how many bones he ate.

✏ **Circle** all the differences that are smaller than 20.

56 – 42 14	39 – 18 21	44 – 21 23	26 – 13 13	67 – 35 32
88 – 15 23	79 – 58 21	59 – 28 31	68 – 47 21	94 – 83 11
32 – 21 11	56 – 15 41	86 – 23 63	74 – 31 43	66 – 52 14

Graphing

Name_____

Count and Color

Count the apples in each row.  **Color** the boxes to show how many apples have bites taken out of them.

Example:

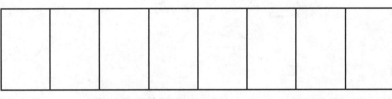

1	2	3	4	5	6	7	8

Name_____

Animal Graph

Make a graph of the animals in the jungle. **Color** one space for each animal.

Name_____

Flower Graph

How many of each color flower are there? **Color** the spaces on the graph below.

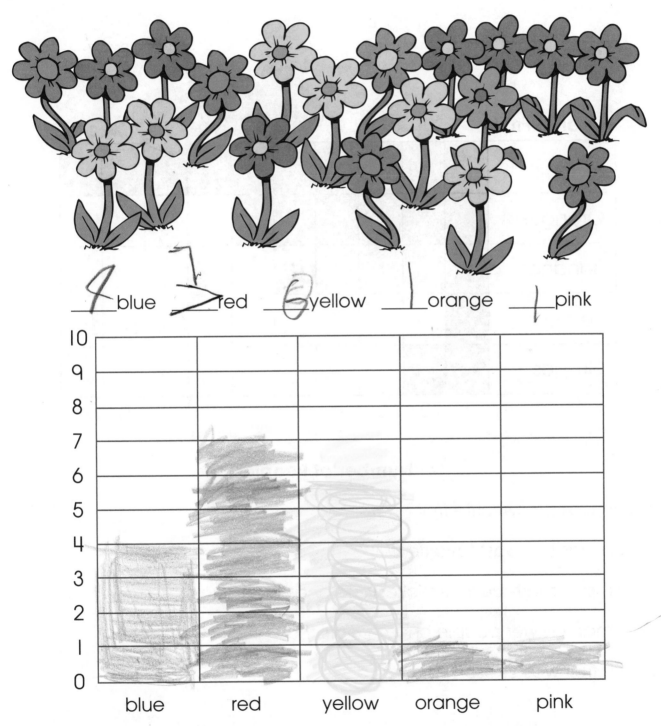

____4 blue   ___2 red   ___6 yellow   ___ orange   ___ pink

Name_____

Fruit Graph

Use the information on the bar graph to **write** the answers to the questions.

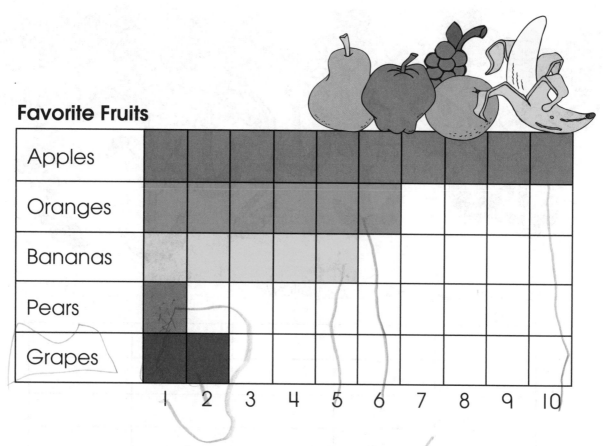

Favorite Fruits

	1	2	3	4	5	6	7	8	9	10
Apples										
Oranges										
Bananas										
Pears										
Grapes										

Number of People

1. Which was the favorite fruit? ___Apples___

2. Which was the least favorite fruit? ___pears___

3. How many more people picked bananas than pears? ___4___

4. How many fewer people chose pears than grapes? ___1___

5. Which fruit was chosen by 6 people? ___oranges___

Name _____

Weather Graph

The pictures show the weather for one month. **Count** the number of sunny, cloudy, and rainy days.

|||| |||| |||| |||| |||| ||||

Then, make a graph with pictures using the tallies above. This kind of graph is called a pictograph.

Weather for 1 month

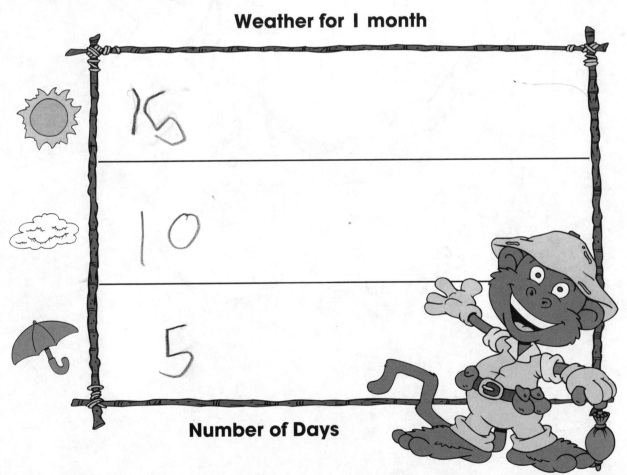

15

10

5

Number of Days

Time

Name_____

Clocks

A clock can tell you what time it is. A clock has different parts. Read and **trace** each part of the clock.

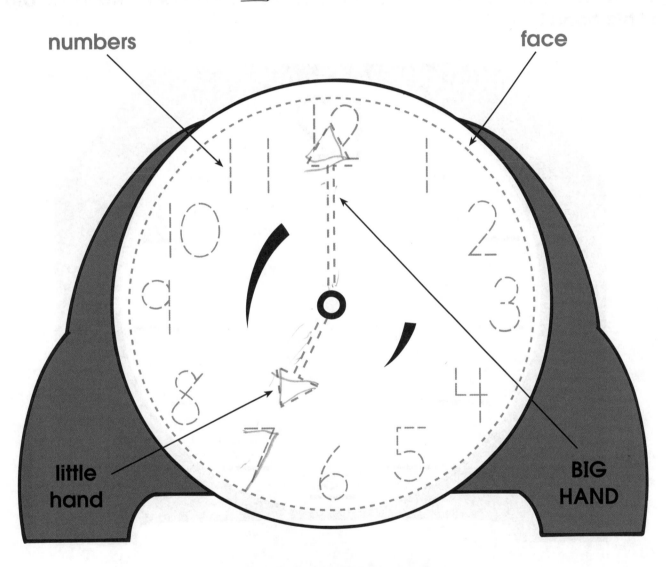

numbers

face

little hand

BIG HAND

The **BIG HAND** is on **12**.
The **little hand** tells the **hour**.

Learning to Tell Time

Learning to tell time is fun! A clock tells us the time.

Write the numbers on the clock face. **Draw** the **BIG HAND** to **12**. **Draw** the **little hand** to **5**.

What time is it? _____5_____ o'clock

Learning to Tell Time

An **hour** is **sixty minutes** long. It takes an **hour** for the **BIG HAND** to go around the clock. When the **BIG HAND** is on **12**, and the **little hand** points to a number, that is the **hour**! The **BIG HAND** is on the **12**.

Color it **red**.   The **little hand** is on the **8**. **Color** it **blue**.

The **BIG HAND** is on _____.

The **little hand** is on _____.

It is _____ o'clock.

Name _____

Little Hour Hand

✏️ **Draw** the **little hour hand** on each clock.

4 o'clock

11 o'clock

5 o'clock

Name_____

Little Hour Hand

Circle the **little hour hand** on each clock. What time is it?

Write the time below.

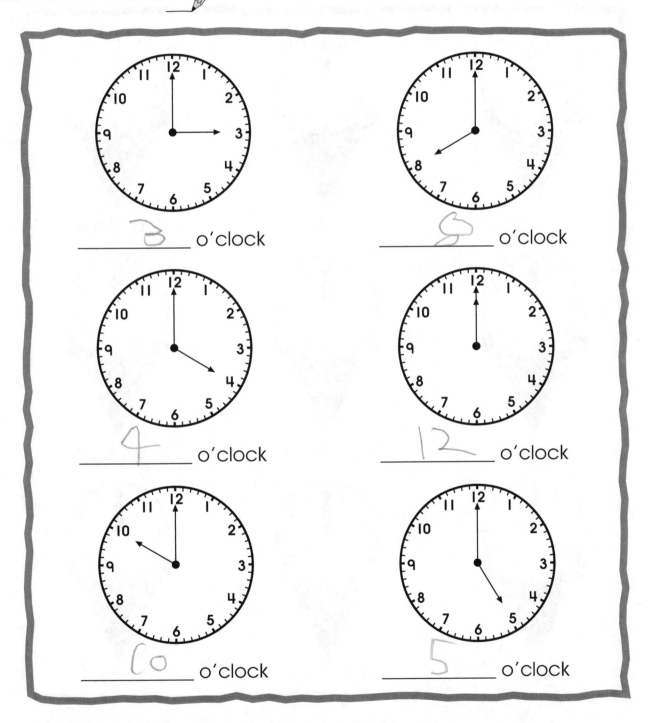

_____3_____ o'clock

_____5_____ o'clock

_____4_____ o'clock

_____12_____ o'clock

_____6_____ o'clock

_____5_____ o'clock

Little Hour Hand

Here's the scoop! _____ **Draw** the **little hour hand** on each clock.

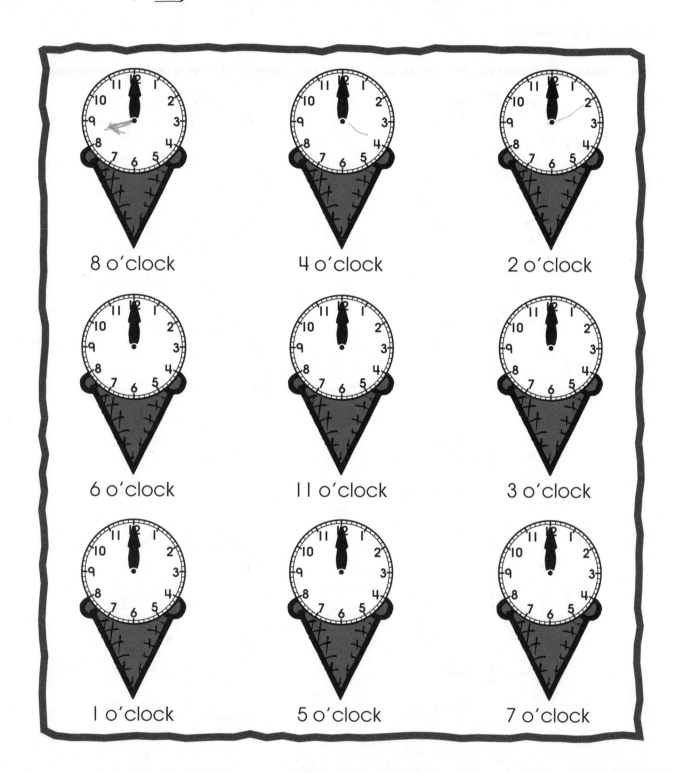

8 o'clock

4 o'clock

2 o'clock

6 o'clock

11 o'clock

3 o'clock

1 o'clock

5 o'clock

7 o'clock

Name _____

What Time is it?

What time is it? ✏️ **Write** the time on each clock in the blanks below.

_____ o'clock   _____ o'clock   _____ o'clock

_____ o'clock   _____ o'clock   _____ o'clock

_____ o'clock   _____ o'clock   _____ o'clock

_____ o'clock   _____ o'clock

Tell Time to the Half Hour

This is how to tell time to the half hour. This clock face shows how much time has gone by since 8 o'clock. **Thirty minutes** or **half an hour** has gone by. There are 3 ways to say time to the half hour. We say **eight-thirty**, **thirty past eight**, or **half past eight**.

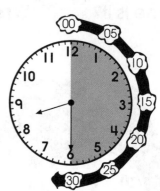

_____ **Write** the time on the clock and the time a half hour later.

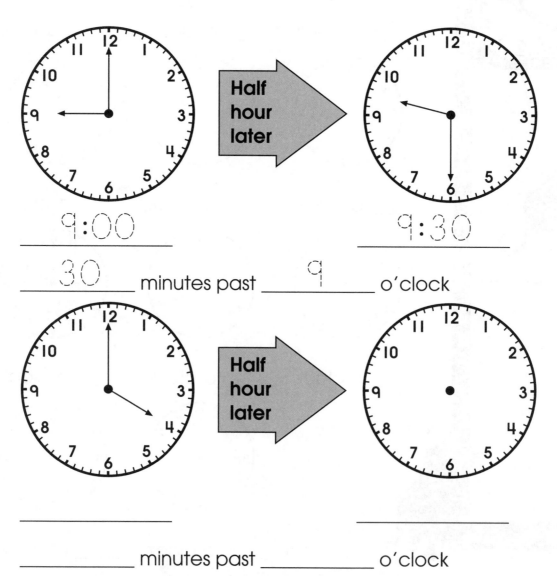

9:00

9:30

30 _____ minutes past _____ 9 _____ o'clock

_____

_____

_____ minutes past _____ o'clock

Write Time to the Half Hour

✏ **Write** the time on the half hour.

   Half hour later ➡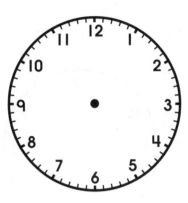

_____   _____

_____ minutes past _____ o'clock

   Half hour later ➡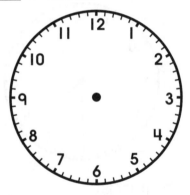

_____   _____

_____ minutes past _____ o'clock

What is your dinner time? ✏ **Circle** the time you eat.

Name_____

What Time is it?

What time is it? **Write** the time on each clock in the blanks below.

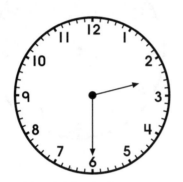

half past _____

half past _____

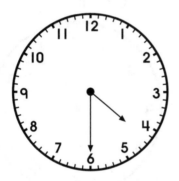

half past _____

half past _____

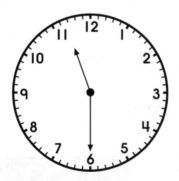

half past _____

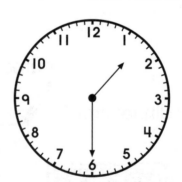

half past _____

Name_____

Big Minute Hand and Little Hour Hand

Trace the **BIG MINUTE HAND** green. **Trace** the **little hour hand** **red**. **Write** the time on the line.

Name_____

Who "Nose" These Times?

Write the time under each clock. **Color** the noses.

_____   _____

_____   _____

_____   _____

Name _____

Digital Numbers

These digital numbers got lost. ✏️ **Write** them on the right clocks on this page and the next page.

6:30	12:30	3:30	8:30	9:30	5:30

Digital Numbers

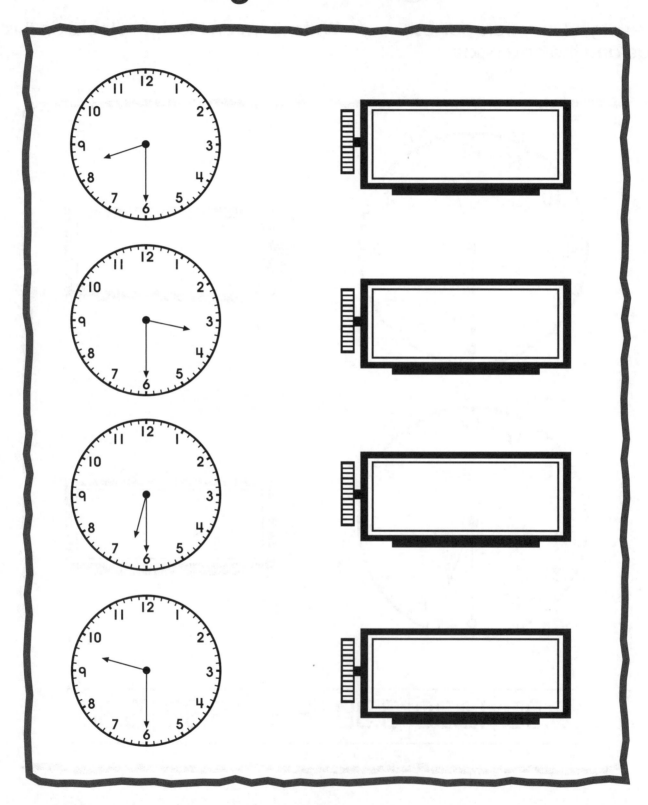

Name_____

Quarter Hour

This is how to tell time to the **quarter hour**.
Each **hour** has **60 minutes**. An **hour** has **4**
quarter hours. A **quarter hour** is **15 minutes**.
This clock face shows a quarter of an hour.

 Trace the numbers below.

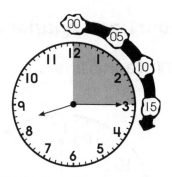

From the **12** to the **3** is **15 minutes**.

_____15_____ minutes after _____8_____ o'clock

is _____8 : 15_____

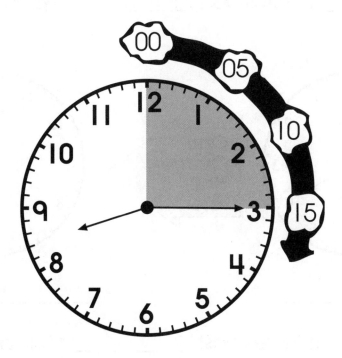

Name_____

Quarter Hour

Each **hour** has **4 quarter hours**. A **quarter hour** is **15 minutes**.

✏ **Write** the times.

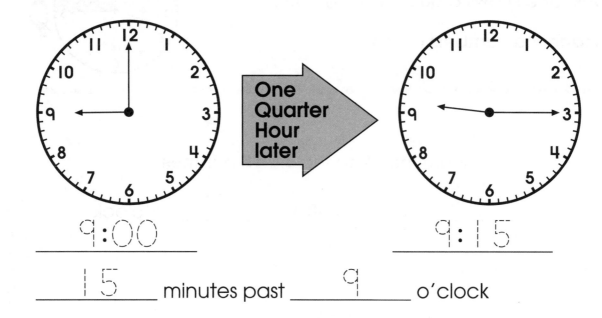

9:00

_____15_____ minutes past _____9_____ o'clock

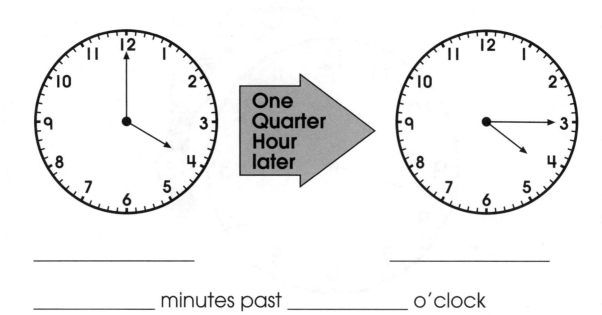

_____   _____

_____ minutes past _____ o'clock

Name_____

Draw the Hands and Write the Time

Draw the hands. **Write** the times.

5:15

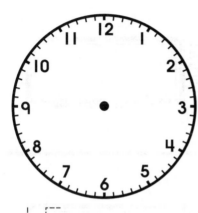

__15__ minutes after

__5__ o'clock

10:15

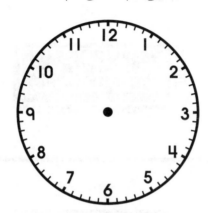

_____ minutes after

_____ o'clock

2:15

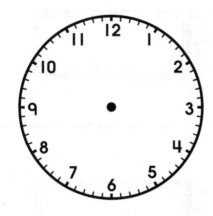

_____ minutes after

_____ o'clock

9:15

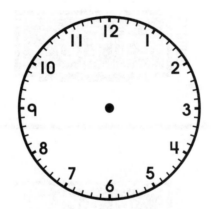

_____ minutes after

_____ o'clock

Name_____

Quarter Hours

Your digital clock has **quarter hours**, too. It also shows **15 minutes**.

Write the time on each digital clock.

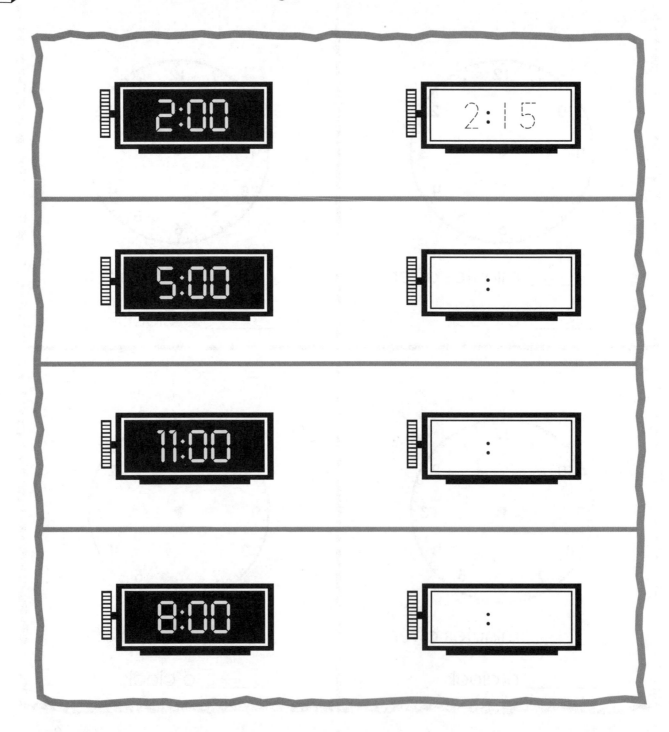

Digital Time

Circle the correct digital time.

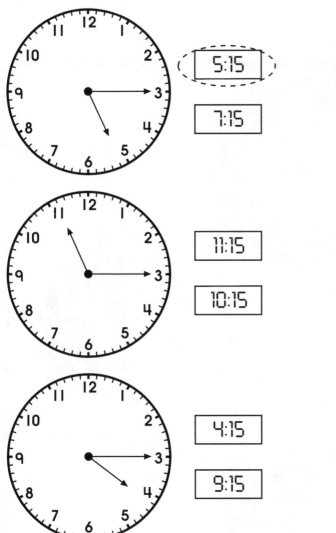

(5:15)

7:15

8:15

10:15

11:15

10:15

2:15

12:15

4:15

9:15

6:15

7:15

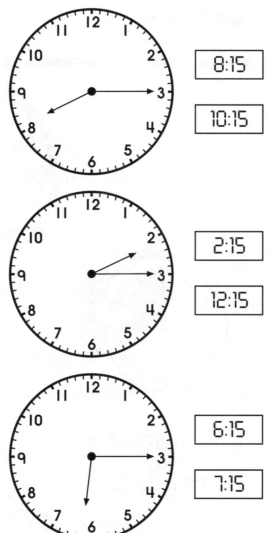

5 minutes past 6 is my dinner time. **Draw** the **minute hand** with an **orange** crayon.

Draw the **hour hand** with a **purple** crayon.

_____ minutes after _____ o'clock

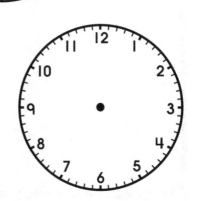

Name_____

Count the Numbers by 5's

Count the numbers by **5's** to see how many minutes have passed.

✏️ **Trace** the numbers.

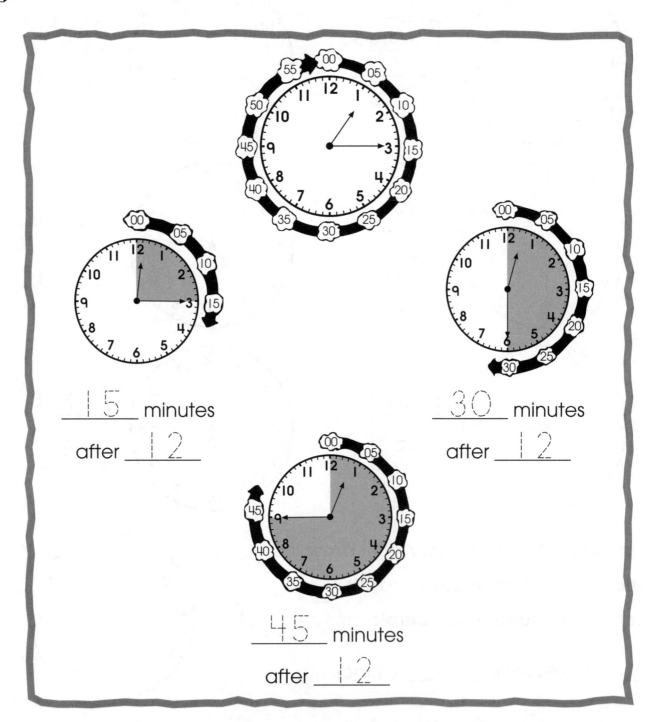

_15_ minutes

after _12_

_30_ minutes

after _12_

_45_ minutes

after _12_

Name_____

Digital Time

Circle the correct digital time.

| 5:15 |
| 7:15 |

| 11:30 |
| 9:30 |

| 10:45 |
| 12:45 |

| 9:45 |
| 3:45 |

| 7:30 |
| 6:45 |

| 10:00 |
| 2:00 |

| 6:15 |
| 6:45 |

| 10:30 |
| 10:45 |

| 4:45 |
| 4:15 |

This pie bakes until
a **quarter past 4**.

Money

Name_____

Money

his is a **penny**.

is worth **I cent**. It has 2 sides.

his is the **cent symbol. Trace** it.

Color the pennies **brown**.

Name_____

Pennies

Count the pennies in each row. **Write** how much.

_____3_____ pennies = _____3_____ ¢

_____ pennies = _____ ¢

_____ penny = _____ ¢

_____ pennies = _____ ¢

_____ pennies = _____ ¢

Name _____

Pennies

 **Write** how much money.

Example:

 = **5** ¢

= 7 ¢

= 4 ¢

= 8 ¢

Pennies

Count how many pennies. 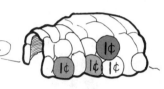 **Write** how many cents.

Example:

    = **4** ¢

        = ☐ ¢

     = ☐ ¢

          = ☐ ¢

    = ☐ ¢

      = ☐ ¢

        = ☐ ¢

  = ☐ ¢

           = ☐ ¢

Name_____

Pennies

Count the pennies on the flowers. ✏️ **Write** how many cents.

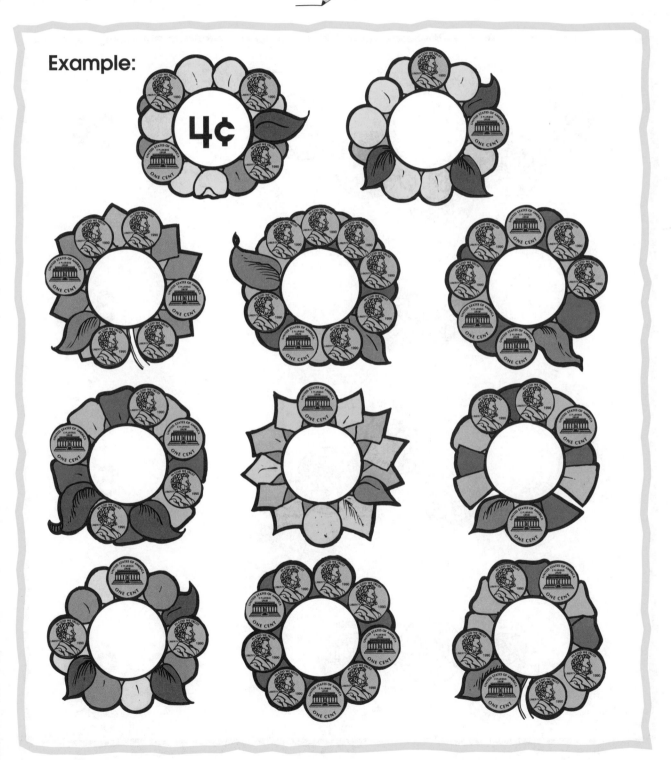

Example:

Name_____

Pennies

Count the pennies in each chain.   **Draw** a line to the number of pennies.

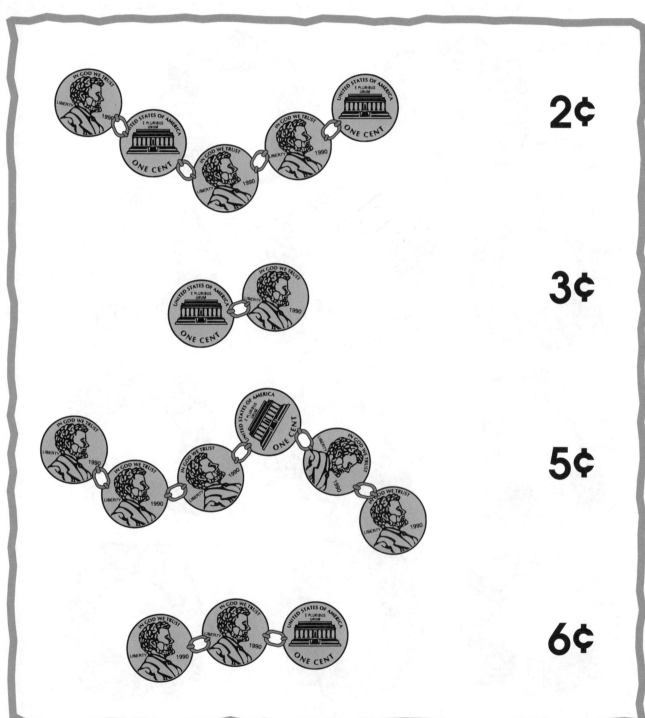

2¢

3¢

5¢

6¢

Name_____

Pennies

Look at the penny pinchers. **Draw** a line from the pennies to the right numbers.

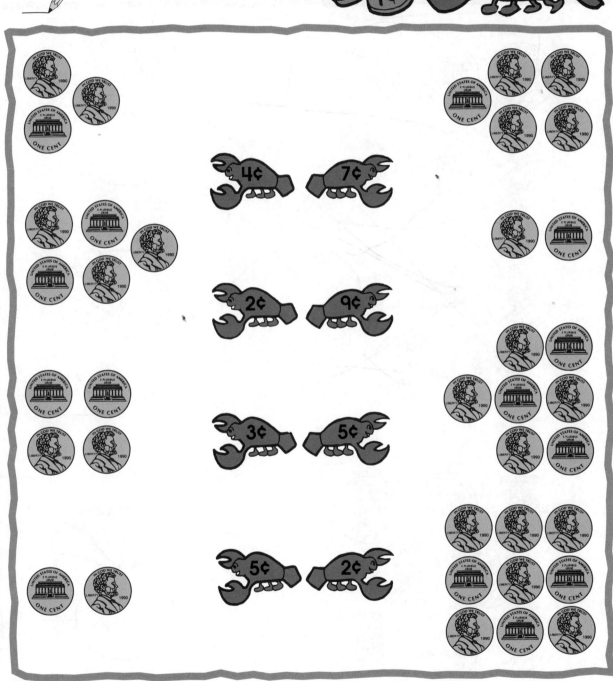

Money

Name_____

Pennies

I put my pennies in bags.
Color each penny.

Write the number of pennies on each bag.

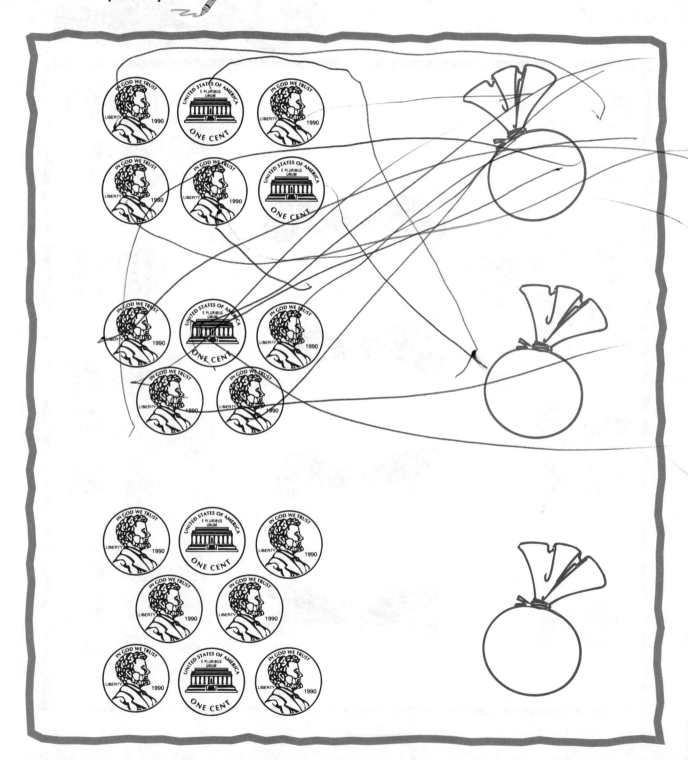

Name_____

Pennies

Count the pennies in each triangle. **Write** the amount.

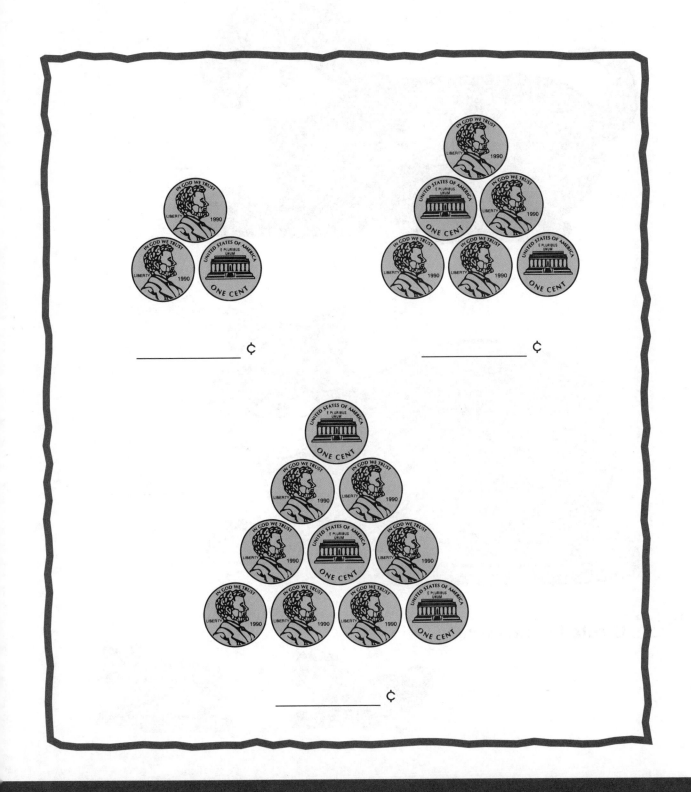

_____ ¢

_____ ¢

_____ ¢

Name_____

Who Has More Money?

Who has more money? **Count** the money. **Write** the amount.

_____ ¢

_____ ¢

Circle the answer.

Nickels

Look at the two sides of a nickel. A nickel is worth **5 cents.** **Trace** the numbers and **write** the number of the cents in the bottom row. **Color** the nickels silver.

_____ nickel   =   _____5_____ pennies

_____ nickel   =   _____5_____ cents

_____ nickel   =   _____5_____ ¢

5¢ = ___1___ ¢ + ___1___ ¢ + ___1___ ¢ + ___1___ ¢ + ___1___ ¢

Name_____

Nickels

Let's **count** the nickels to see if there are enough to buy something!
Count by **5's**. See how far you can count.

_____5_____ , _____10_____ , _____15_____ , _____20_____ , _____25_____ ,

_____30_____ , _____35_____ , _____40_____ , _____45_____ , _____50_____ ,

_____55_____ , _____60_____ , _____65_____ , _____70_____ , _____75_____ ,

_____80_____ , _____85_____ , _____90_____ , _____95_____ , _____100_____

That is how you count nickels!

Practice counting by **5's**!

Name_____

Nickels

Each **nickel** is worth **5 cents**. **Write** how much these nickels are worth.
Remember to count by **5's**.

 = _____ ¢

 = _____ ¢

= _____ ¢   = _____ ¢

 = _____ ¢

= _____ ¢

= _____ ¢   = _____ ¢

 = _____ ¢

= _____ ¢

= _____ ¢

= _____ ¢   = _____ ¢

Nickels

You can buy a pickle for a nickel. **Count** the nickels by **5's**.

 **Write** the amount.

5 cents = 1 nickel

 ⬜ ¢

Count __5__, __10__, __15__.

  ⬜ ¢

Count _____, _____.

 ⬜ ¢

Count _____, _____, _____,

_____, _____.

 ⬜ ¢

Count _____, _____, _____, _____,

_____, _____, _____.

⬜ ¢

Count _____, _____,

_____, _____.

 ⬜ ¢

Count _____, _____, _____,

_____, _____, _____.

Name_____

Hive of Five

How much money is in each hive of five? _____ **Count** by **5's** and **write** the amount of money.

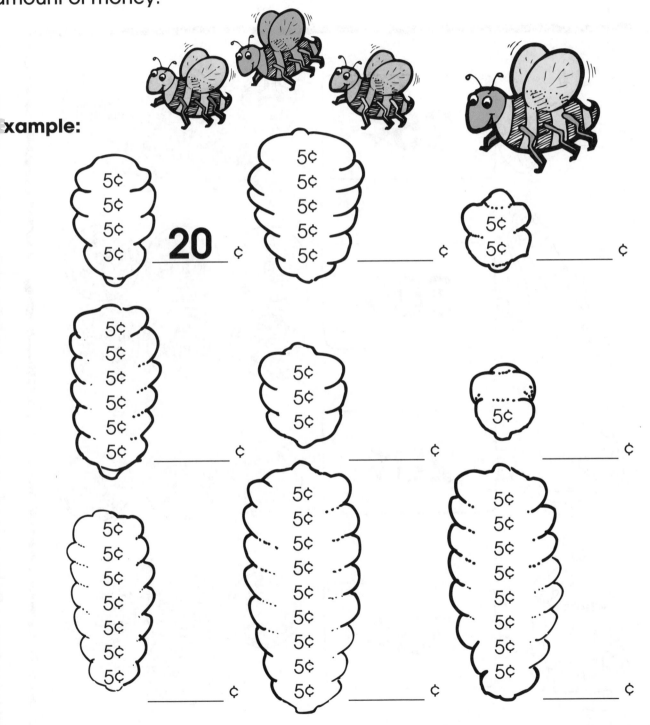

Example:

20 ¢

Price of Each Toy

Look at the price on each toy. 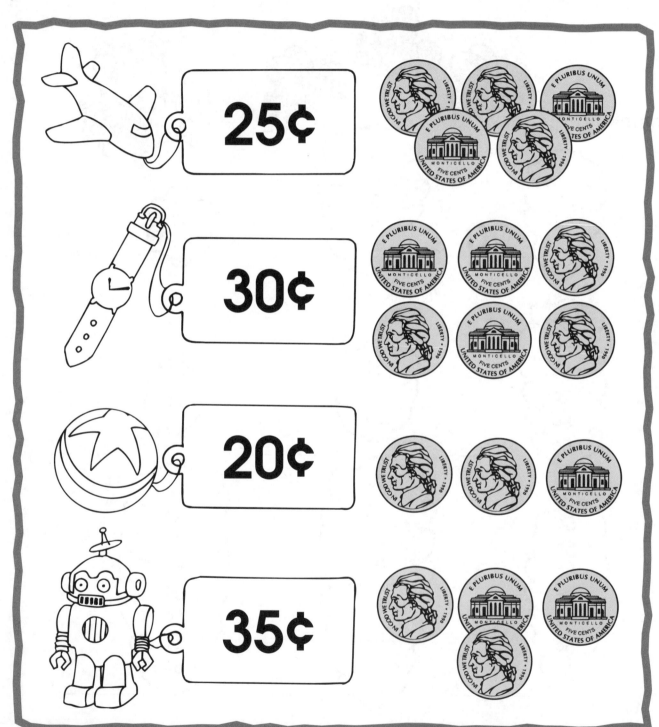 **Color** it if there are enough nickels to buy it.

Name_____

Count the Nickels

Count the nickels. ✏️ **Write** the amount of money in each meter.

Example:

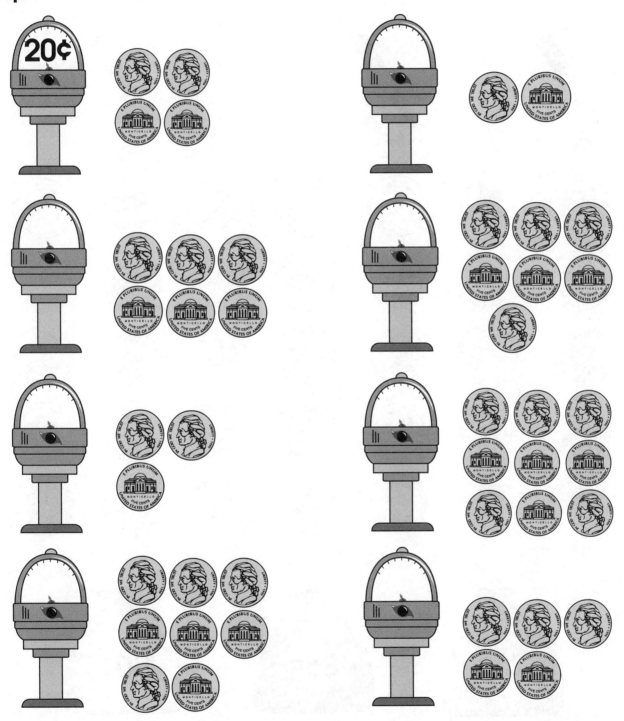

Name_____

Count by 5's

Count by **5's.** **Color** the correct number of nickels for each bag.

Begin at the star. Watch out for the pennies!

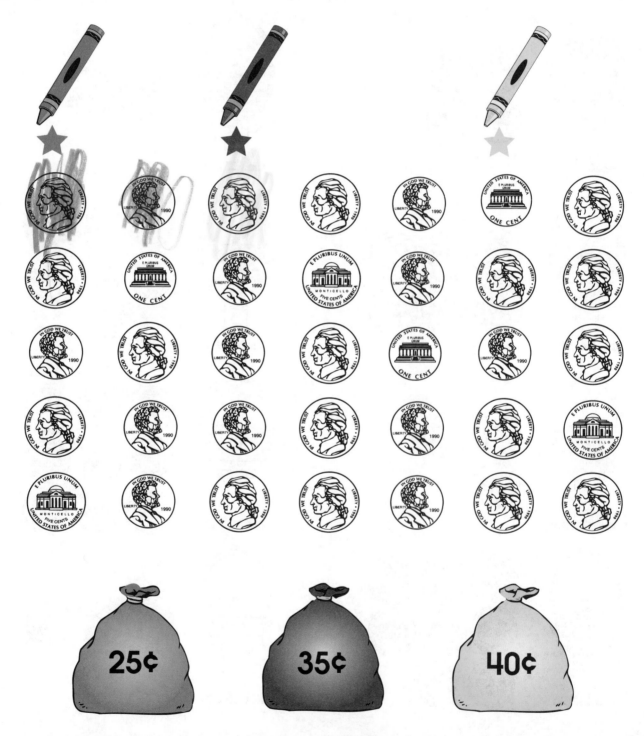

Name_____

Count the Coins

Count the coins on each "cent"-erpillar.

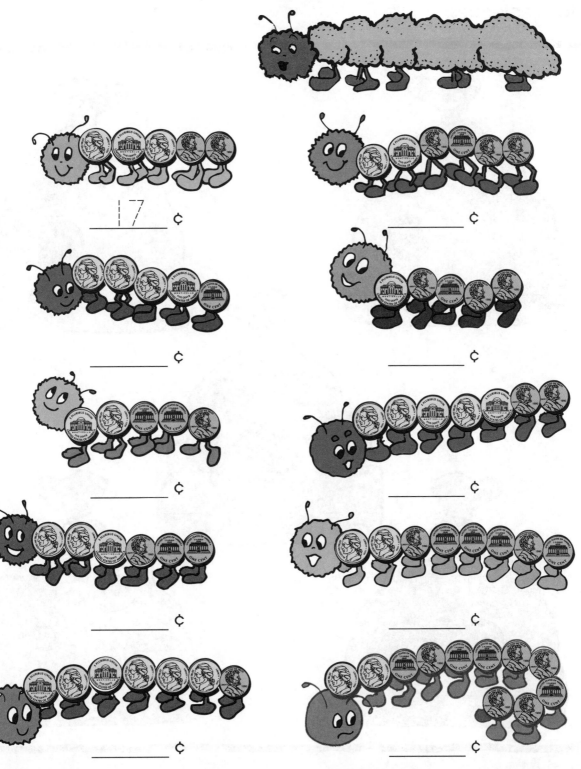

17 ¢

_____ ¢

_____ ¢

_____ ¢

_____ ¢

_____ ¢

_____ ¢

_____ ¢

_____ ¢

_____ ¢

Name_____

Count the Coins

Count the coins. ✏️ **Write** numbers in the blanks to complete the addition sentences.

_5_ ¢ + _1_ ¢ =_____

_____ ¢ + _____ ¢ =_____

_____ ¢ + _____ ¢ =_____

_____ ¢ + _____ ¢ =_____

_____ ¢ + _____ ¢ =_____

Name _____

Dimes

Look at the two sides of a **dime**. A **dime** is worth **10 cents**.

front   back

Each side of a dime is different. It has ridges on its edge.  **Color** the dime **silver**.

 =

_____ dime = _____ pennies

_____ dime = _____ cents

_____ dime = _____ ¢

Name_____

Count by 10's

Count by **10's**. ✏️ **Write** the number. ✏️ **Circle** the group with more.

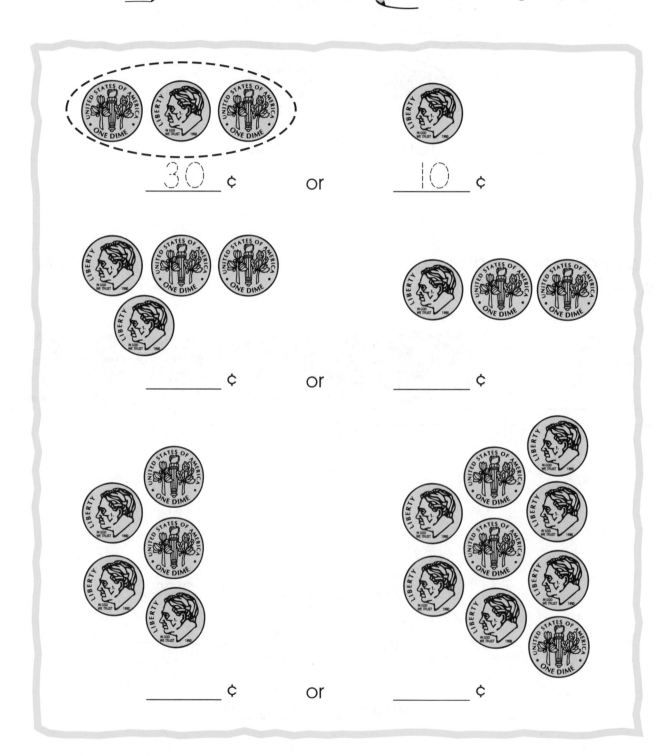

_30_ ¢   or   _10_ ¢

_____ ¢   or   _____ ¢

_____ ¢   or   _____ ¢

Name_____

Dimes and Pennies

Count the dimes and the pennies.

Say __10__ __11__ __12__ = __12__ ¢
  Total

Begin with the dime, then **add** the pennies.

 Write the amount.

_____ _____ _____ _____ = _____ ¢

_____ _____ = _____ ¢

_____

_____ _____ _____ = _____ ¢

Name_____

Count the Money

Count the money. **Count** the dimes, then **count** the nickels.

Write the amount.

_____¢ _____¢ _____¢ _____¢ _____¢ _____¢ Total

_____¢ _____¢ _____¢ _____¢ _____¢ _____¢

_____¢ _____¢ _____¢ _____¢ Total

Solve this puzzle.

What coins does Raccoon have?

 Draw them here.

I'm counting my money. 10¢, 20¢, 30¢, 35¢, 40¢, 45¢, 50¢...

Count the Dimes, Nickels, Pennies

Count the dimes, the nickels, and the pennies. **Write** how many cents.

    _____ ¢

   _____ ¢

  _____ ¢

If you add 1 more penny to the first row, you will have _____ ¢

If you add 1 more penny to the second row, you will have _____ ¢

If you add 1 more penny to the third row, you will have _____ ¢

To count these cents takes a lot of sense!

Name_____

Count the Money

Count the money. Start with the dimes. Then, count the nickels and the pennies. _____ **Write** your answer on the "Total" line.

_____ ¢   _____ ¢   _____ ¢   _____ ¢   _____ ¢   _____ ¢
                                                              Total

_____ ¢   _____ ¢   _____ ¢   _____ ¢

_____ ¢   _____ ¢   _____ ¢   _____ ¢
                              Total

Name_____

Count the Money

Count the money. **Write** each amount on the line.

penny

__1__ ¢

nickel

__5__ ¢

dime

__10__ ¢

Example:

__10__ ¢ __10__ ¢ __1__ ¢ __1__ ¢ = __22__ ¢

____ ¢ ____ ¢ ____ ¢ ____ ¢ ____ ¢ ____ ¢ = ____ ¢

____ ¢ ____ ¢ ____ ¢ ____ ¢ ____ ¢ ____ ¢ = ____ ¢

____ ¢ ____ ¢ ____ ¢ ____ ¢ ____ ¢ = ____ ¢

____ ¢ ____ ¢ ____ ¢ ____ ¢ ____ ¢ = ____ ¢

____ ¢ ____ ¢ ____ ¢ ____ ¢ ____ ¢ ____ ¢ = ____ ¢

Name_____

Bake Sale

There is a bake sale at school today. Take some money with you!

Decide which one you want. In the space below, draw enough money to pay for it.

Name_____

Bake Sale

At the bake sale, Sharita chose the donut. Look at the previous page.

Circle the money she needed.

_____ ¢

Robert loves brownies.

Circle the money he needed.

_____ ¢

Tom had 3 of these.

He had _____ ¢. He spent it all on something good.

Draw it here.

Name_____

Quarters

Here is a **quarter**. Our first President, George Washington, is on the front. The American eagle is on the **back**. A **quarter** is worth **25 cents**.

front

back

_____1_____ quarter = _____25_____ pennies

_____1_____ quarter = _____25_____ cents

_____1_____ quarter = _____25_____ ¢

Count these nickels by **5's**. Is this another way to make 25¢?

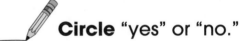 **Circle** "yes" or "no."

yes   no

Name_____

Quarters

These are all ways to make **25¢.**

Color each coin.

I quarter

5 nickels

2 dimes,
I nickel

25
pennies

Name_____

Quarters

It costs 25¢ to catch a fish. **Circle** each group of coins that makes 25¢.
Do not circle any coin more than once. How many fish can I catch?

 Draw and **color** the number of fish I can catch.

Name_____

Buying Fruit

Patty bought these pears at the store. She paid **25¢** for each pear.

Color the pears.

 Draw the quarters she spent.

How much did she spend? _____ ¢

Jennifer bought these bananas. She paid **10¢** for each one.

Color the bananas.

 Draw the dimes she spent.

How much did she spend? _____ ¢

Which girl spent less? _____

Name_____

Count the Money

Count the money. **Write** the amount.

_____ ¢   _____ ¢   _____ ¢   _____ ¢
Total

_____ ¢   _____ ¢   _____ ¢   _____ ¢
Total

Put more than 50¢ in the bank. **Draw** the coins.

Count the Money

Count the money. Start with the quarters. Then, **count** the dimes, the nickels, and the pennies.

_____ ¢ _____ ¢ _____ ¢ _____ ¢ _____ ¢ _____ ¢
                                                        Total

_____ ¢ _____ ¢ _____ ¢ _____ ¢ _____ ¢ _____ ¢

_____ ¢ _____ ¢ _____ ¢
              Total
_____

Solve this puzzle. What coins

does Lizard have? **Write**

the number of each coin.

_____

_____

I'm counting my money. 25¢, 35¢, 45¢, 55¢, 60¢, 65¢, 66¢, 67¢.

Name_____

Count the Coins

Count the coins. Start with the quarters. **Write** the amount in each football.

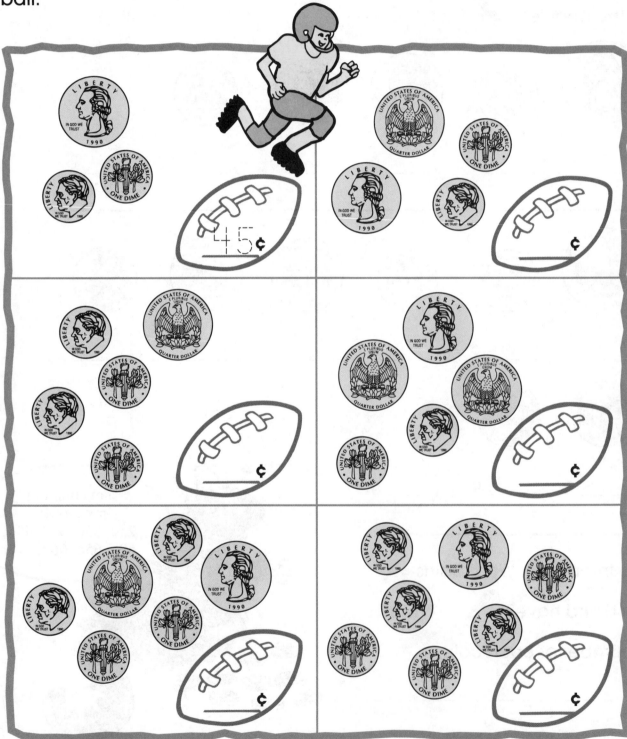

Number Rhymes and Activities

For Parents, Caregivers, and Educators

This section includes songs, rhymes, and activities for children that teach and reinforce numbers to 100 in creative and playful ways. You may wish to sing the rhyme to a familiar tune to make learning easier and more fun, or have the children make up a tune together.

These are several counting activities for each number through 10. The songs, rhymes, and activities include a variety of curriculum areas such as language, math, music, and movement. Many of these activities can serve as springboards to other ideas. You may think of another or better way of presenting a certain number. Encourage the children to follow along while you read and act out the activity. For example, for "Five Little Cookies," you may wish to use five flannel cookie shapes on a flannelboard and have children take away one "cookie" at a time as you say the verse. Children will also enjoy acting out "Bears on the Train."

If some of the activities appear to be too juvenile for the children that you are working with, encourage them to lead a younger sibling or friend with the verses. This will help reinforce numbers and counting for the child leading the activities.

Although these songs, rhymes, and activities are educational, they are also fun. Enjoy each activity with the children as you work with them to learn their numbers and counting.

Name_____

Five Little Cookies

Five little cookies by the door

Mother ate one.
Now there are four.

Four little cookies by the tree

Father ate one.
Now there are three.

Three little cookies by the shoe

Sister ate one.
Now there are two.

Two little cookies just got done

Brother ate one.
Now there is one.

One little cookie, the only one

I ate it.
Now there are none.

Six Days of Summer

On the first day
of summer,
What did I see?

A robin up in a tree.

On the second day
of summer,
What did I see?

Two ducks swimming
And a robin up in a tree.

On the thrid day
of summer,
What did I see?

Three bees buzzing,
Two ducks swimming,
And a robin up in a tree.

On the fourth day
of summer,
What did I see?

Four dogs barking,
Three bees buzzing,
Two ducks swimming,
And a robin up in a tree.

On the fifth day
of summer,
What did I see?

Five picnic baskets,
Four dogs barking,
Three bees buzzing,
Two ducks swimming,
And a robin up in a tree.

On the sixth day
of summer,
What did I see?

Six flowers growing,
Five picnic baskets,
Four dogs barking,
Three bees buzzing,
Two ducks swimming,
And a robin up in a tree.

Ten Little Bunnies

Ten little bunnies jumping on the bed,

One fell off and bumped her head.
How many bunnies
Jumping on the bed? _____

Nine little bunnies jumping on the bed,

One fell off and bumped her head.
How many bunnies
Jumping on the bed? _____

Eight little bunnies jumping on the bed,

One fell off and bumped her head.
How many bunnies
Jumping on the bed? _____

Seven little bunnies jumping on the bed,

One fell off and bumped her head.
How many bunnies
Jumping on the bed? _____

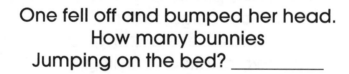

Six little bunnies jumping on the bed,

One fell off and bumped her head.
How many bunnies
Jumping on the bed? _____

Five little bunnies jumping on the bed,

One fell off and bumped her head.
How many bunnies
Jumping on the bed? _____

Ten Little Bunnies

Four little bunnies jumping on the bed,

One fell off and bumped her head.
How many bunnies
Jumping on the bed? _____

Three little bunnies jumping on the bed,

One fell off and bumped her head.
How many bunnies
Jumping on the bed? _____

Two little bunnies jumping on the bed,

One fell off and bumped her head.
How many bunnies
Jumping on the bed? _____

One little bunny jumping on the bed,

He fell off and bumped his head.
How many bunnies
Jumping on the bed? _____

Ten little bunnies lying on the floor.
"Get back to bed and jump no more!"

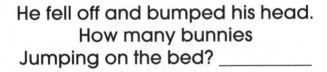

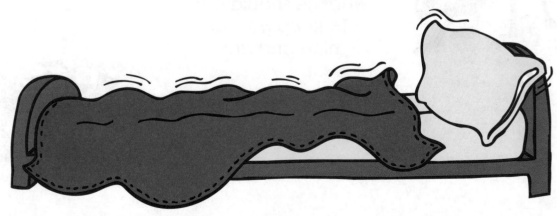

Boots For Sale

How many boots
should the little duck buy
To keep his feet
nice and dry? _____

Two little boots is
what he should buy
To keep his feet
nice and dry.

How many boots
should the little cat buy
To keep her feet
nice and dry? _____

Four little boots is
what she should buy
To keep her feet
nice and dry.

How many boots
should the little duck buy
To keep his feet
nice and dry? _____

Six little boots is
what he should buy
To keep his feet
nice and dry.

Name_____

Boots For Sale

How many boots
should the little pig buy
To keep her feet
nice and dry? _____

Four little boots is
what she should buy
To keep her feet
nice and dry.

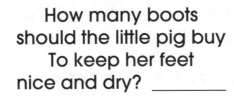

How many boots
should the little crab buy
To keep his feet
nice and dry? _____

Eight little boots is
what he should buy
To keep his feet
nice and dry.

How many boots
should the little fish buy
To keep her feet
nice and dry? _____

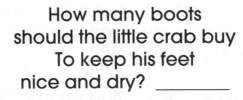

Zero little boots is
what she should buy
To keep her feet
nice and dry.

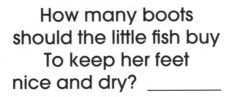

Bears On The Train

Ten little bears riding on the train
Looks like it is going to rain.

Two little bears get off the train.
How many bears are now
Riding on the train? _____

Eight little bears riding on the train
Looks like it is going to rain.

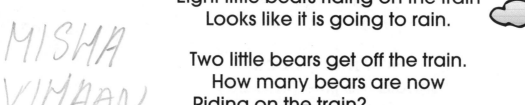

Two little bears get off the train.
How many bears are now
Riding on the train? _____

Six little bears riding on the train
Looks like it is going to rain.

Two little bears get off the train.
How many bears are now
Riding on the train? _____

Name_____

Bears On The Train

Four little bears riding on the train
Looks like it is going to rain.

Two little bears get off the train.
How many bears are now
Riding on the train? _____

Two little bears riding on the train
Looks like it is going to rain.

Two little bears get off the train.
How many bears are now
Riding on the train? _____

Zero bears riding on the train
Crash! Boom!
Down comes the rain!

Name_____

On The Pond

One little girl rowing in the pond,

Another girl comes along.
How many girls are now
Rowing on the pond? _____

Two little birds flying over the pond,

Two more birds come along.
How many birds are now
Flying over the pond? _____

Three little fish
Swimming in the pond,

Another fish comes along.
How many fish are now
Swimming in the pond? _____

Four little ducks
Swimming in the pond,

Another duck comes along.
How many ducks are now
Swimming in the pond? _____

Five little butterflies
Flying over the pond,

Another butterfly comes along.
How many butterflies are now
Flying over the pond? _____

Challenge:
How many are there altogether?

_____

Page 16

Page 17

Page 18

Page 24

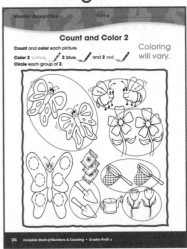

Page 25

Page 26

Page 32

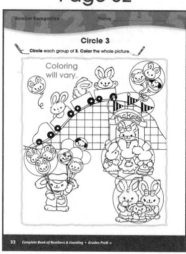

Page 33

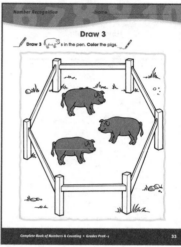

Page 34

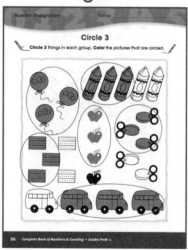

Page 40

Page 41

Page 42

Page 48

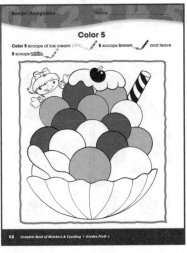

Page 49

Page 50

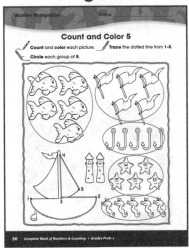

Page 52

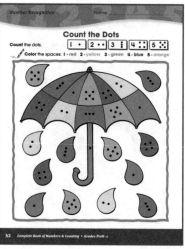

Page 53

Page 54

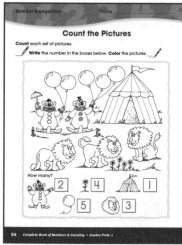

Page 55

Page 56

Page 57

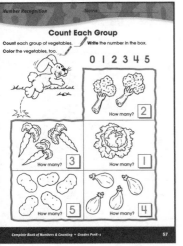

Count Each Group

Count each group of vegetables. Write the number in the box.
Color the vegetables, too.

0 1 2 3 4 5

How many? 2
How many? 3
How many? 1
How many? 5
How many? 4

Complete Book of Numbers & Counting • Grades PreK–1   57

Page 58

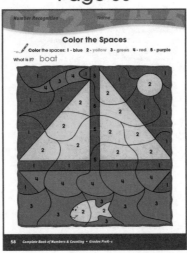

Color the Spaces

Color the spaces: 1 - blue 2 - yellow 3 - green 4 - red 5 - purple

What is it? boat

58   Complete Book of Numbers & Counting • Grades PreK–1

Page 59

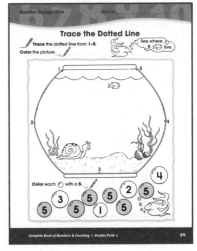

Trace the Dotted Line

Trace the dotted line from 1–5.
Color the picture.

See where 5 live.

Color each with a 5.

5 3 5 5 2 5
5 5 1 5

Complete Book of Numbers & Counting • Grades PreK–1   59

Page 60

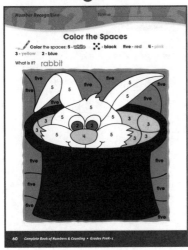

Color the Spaces

Color the spaces: 5 - white - black five - red 4 - pink
3 - yellow 2 - blue

What is it? rabbit

60   Complete Book of Numbers & Counting • Grades PreK–1

Page 61

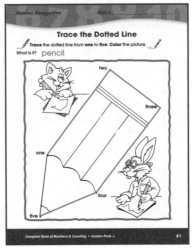

Trace the Dotted Line

Trace the dotted line from one to five. Color the picture.
What is it? pencil

two
three
one
four
five

Complete Book of Numbers & Counting • Grades PreK–1   61

Page 62

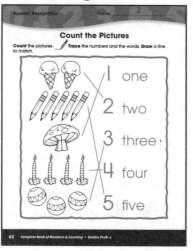

Page 63

Page 64

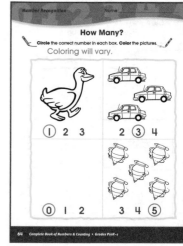

Page 65

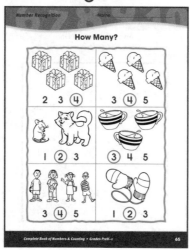

Page 66

Page 72

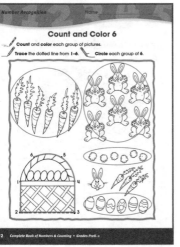

Page 73

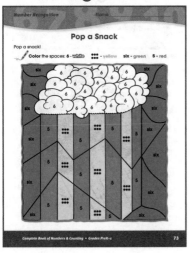

Page 74

Page 80

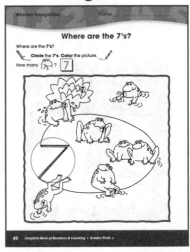

Page 81

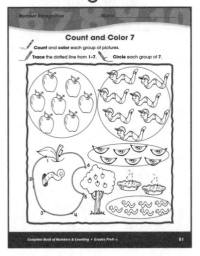

Page 82

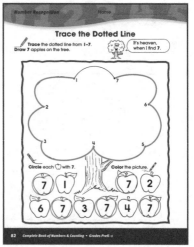

Page 88

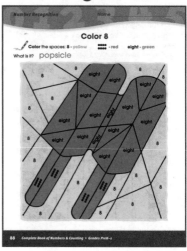

Page 89

Page 95

Page 96

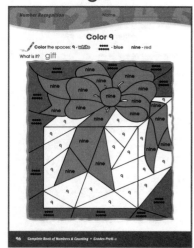

Page 102

Page 103

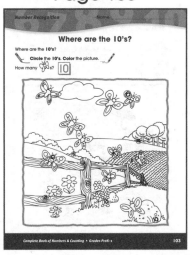

Page 106

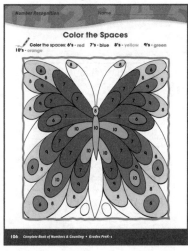

Page 107

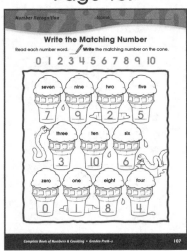

Page 108

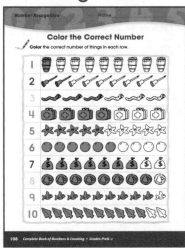

Answer Key

Page 109

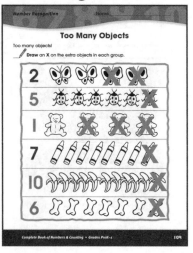

Page 110

Page 111

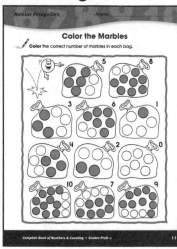

Page 112

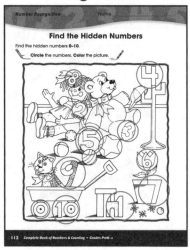

Page 113

Page 114

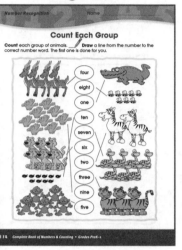

Page 115

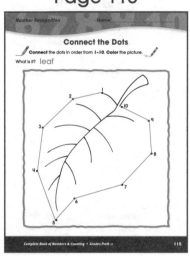

Page 116

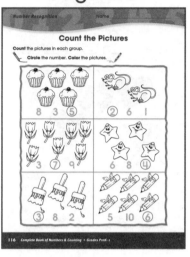

Page 117

Page 118

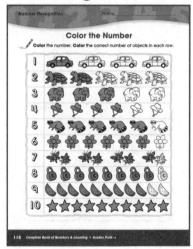

Page 119

Page 120

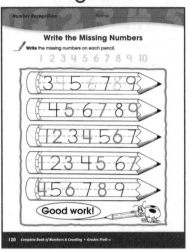

Page 121

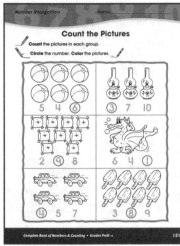

Page 122

Page 123

Page 124

Page 125

Page 131

Page 137

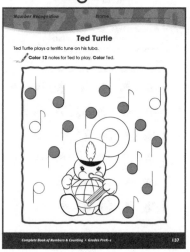

Page 138

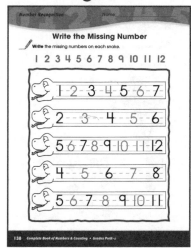

Page 144

Page 150

Page 151

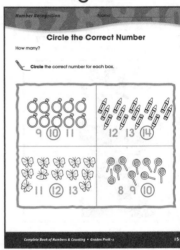

Page 157

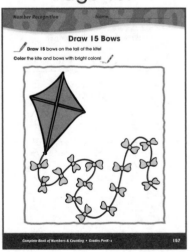

Page 158

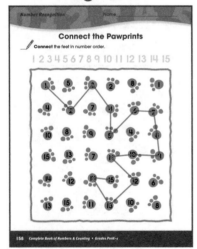

Page 164

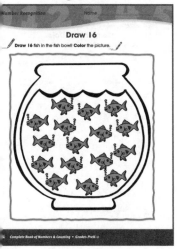

Page 170

Page 176

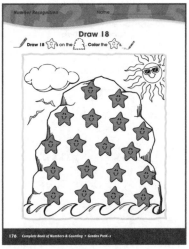

Page 182

Page 188

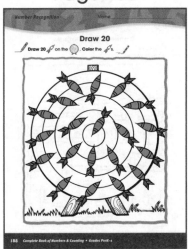

Page 191

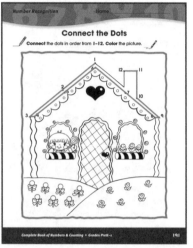

Page 192

Page 193

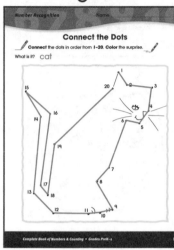

Page 194

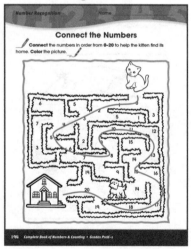

Page 195

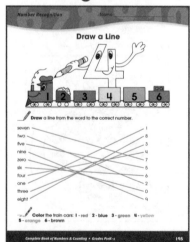

Page 196

Page 197

Page 198

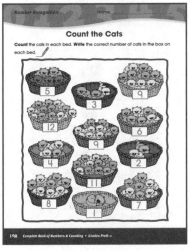

Page 201

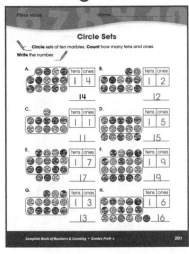

Page 202

Page 203

Use the Numbers

Use the numbers on the left of the charts to **write** in the ones place to see how numbers **20–29** are made. The number in the tens place stays the same for all ten numbers.

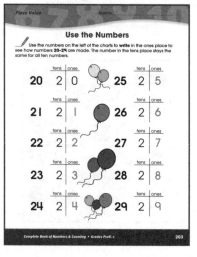

	tens	ones			tens	ones
20	2	0		**25**	2	5
21	2	1		**26**	2	6
22	2	2		**27**	2	7
23	2	3		**28**	2	8
24	2	4		**29**	2	9

Page 204

Use the Numbers

Use the numbers on the left of the charts to **write** in the ones place to see how numbers **30–39** are made. The number in the tens place stays the same for all ten numbers.

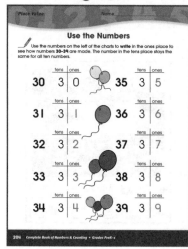

	tens	ones			tens	ones
30	3	0		**35**	3	5
31	3	1		**36**	3	6
32	3	2		**37**	3	7
33	3	3		**38**	3	8
34	3	4		**39**	3	9

Page 205

Use the Numbers

Use the numbers on the left of the charts to **write** in the ones place to see how numbers **40–49** are made. The number in the tens place stays the same for all ten numbers.

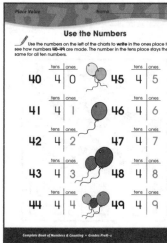

	tens	ones			tens	ones
40	4	0		**45**	4	5
41	4	1		**46**	4	6
42	4	2		**47**	4	7
43	4	3		**48**	4	8
44	4	4		**49**	4	9

Page 207

Connect the Dots

Connect the dots in order from **1–50**. **Color** the creature.

What is it?

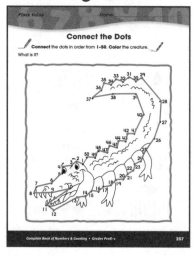

Page 208

Use the Numbers

Use the numbers on the left of the charts to **write** in the ones place to see how numbers **50–54** are made. The number in the tens place stays the same for all ten numbers.

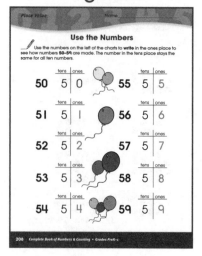

	tens	ones			tens	ones
50	5	0		**55**	5	5
51	5	1		**56**	5	6
52	5	2		**57**	5	7
53	5	3		**58**	5	8
54	5	4		**59**	5	9

Page 209

Use the Numbers

Use the numbers on the left of the charts to **write** in the ones place to see how numbers **60–69** are made. The number in the tens place stays the same for all ten numbers.

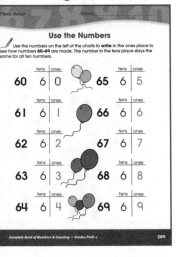

	tens	ones			tens	ones
60	6	0		65	6	5
61	6	1		66	6	6
62	6	2		67	6	7
63	6	3		68	6	8
64	6	4		69	6	9

Complete Book of Numbers & Counting • Grades PreK–1   209

Page 210

Use the Numbers

Use the numbers on the left of the charts to **write** in the ones place to see how numbers **70–79** are made. The number in the tens place stays the same for all ten numbers.

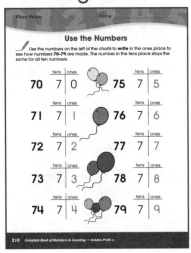

	tens	ones			tens	ones
70	7	0		75	7	5
71	7	1		76	7	6
72	7	2		77	7	7
73	7	3		78	7	8
74	7	4		79	7	9

210   Complete Book of Numbers & Counting • Grades PreK–1

Page 211

Use the Numbers

Use the numbers on the left of the charts to **write** in the ones place to see how numbers **80–89** are made. The number in the tens place stays the same for all ten numbers.

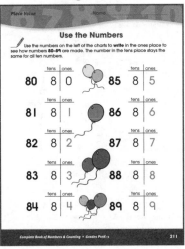

	tens	ones			tens	ones
80	8	0		85	8	5
81	8	1		86	8	6
82	8	2		87	8	7
83	8	3		88	8	8
84	8	4		89	8	9

Complete Book of Numbers & Counting • Grades PreK–1   211

Page 212

Use the Numbers

Use the numbers on the left of the charts to **write** in the ones place to see how numbers **90–99** are made. The number in the tens place stays the same for all ten numbers.

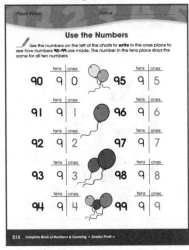

	tens	ones			tens	ones
90	9	0		95	9	5
91	9	1		96	9	6
92	9	2		97	9	7
93	9	3		98	9	8
94	9	4		99	9	9

212   Complete Book of Numbers & Counting • Grades PreK–1

Page 213

Use the Place Value Chart

Use the place value chart to build each number.   **Write** the numbers in the table.

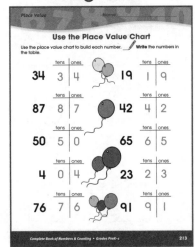

	tens	ones			tens	ones
34	3	4		19	1	9
87	8	7		42	4	2
50	5	0		65	6	5
4	0	4		23	2	3
76	7	6		91	9	1

Complete Book of Numbers & Counting • Grades PreK–1   213

Page 214

Place Value   Name

Write the Value

Write the value of each number below.

35 __3__ tens __5__ ones
19 __1__ tens __9__ ones
8   __0__ tens __8__ ones
26 __2__ tens __6__ ones
49 __4__ tens __9__ ones
10 __1__ tens __0__ ones

Write the numbers below.

4 tens 6 ones __46__   3 tens 2 ones __32__
2 tens 9 ones __29__   4 tens 0 ones __40__
1 ten 4 ones __14__   0 tens 6 ones __6__
2 tens 1 one __21__   4 tens 7 ones __47__
3 tens 3 ones __33__   1 ten 1 one __11__

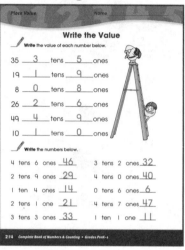

214 Complete Book of Numbers & Counting • Grades PreK–1

Page 215

Place Value   Name

Add the Ones and the Tens

Add the ones and tens.   Write the answer on the blank.

Example:

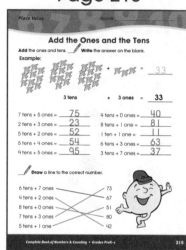

3 tens   +   3 ones   =   **33**

7 tens + 5 ones = __75__   4 tens + 0 ones = __40__
2 tens + 3 ones = __23__   8 tens + 1 one = __81__
5 tens + 2 ones = __52__   1 ten + 1 one = __11__
5 tens + 4 ones = __54__   6 tens + 3 ones = __63__
9 tens + 5 ones = __95__   3 tens + 7 ones = __37__

Draw a line to the correct number.

6 tens + 7 ones   73
4 tens + 2 ones   67
8 tens + 0 ones   51
7 tens + 3 ones   80
5 tens + 1 one   42

Complete Book of Numbers & Counting • Grades PreK–1   215

Page 217

Place Value   Name

Color 30–69

Color the ball red if the number is 30–39.   Color the ball purple
if the number is 40–49.   Color the ball blue if the number is 50–59.
Color the ball green if the number is 60–69.

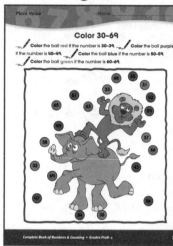

Complete Book of Numbers & Counting • Grades PreK–1

Page 218

Place Value   Name

Connect the Dots

Connect the dots in order from 1–75. Color the animal.

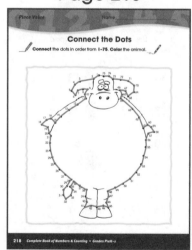

218 Complete Book of Numbers & Counting • Grades PreK–1

Page 219

Place Value   Name

Color the Bubbles

Color the bubble red if the number is 1–25.   Color the bubble
orange if the number is 26–50.   Color the bubble yellow if the
number is 51–75.   Color the bubble blue if the number is 76–100.

Complete Book of Numbers & Counting • Grades PreK–1   219

Page 221

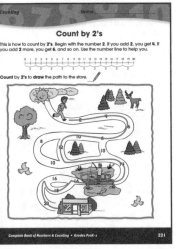

Page 222

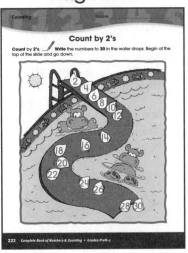

Page 223

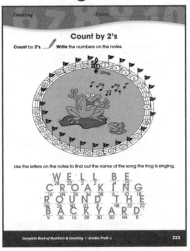

Page 224

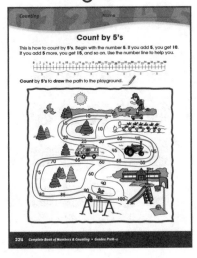

Page 225

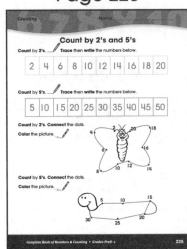

Answer Key

Page 226

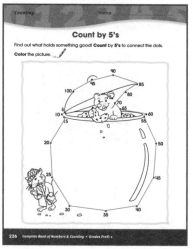

Page 227

Page 228

Page 229

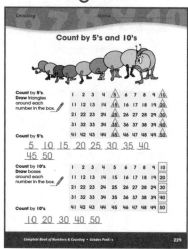

Page 230

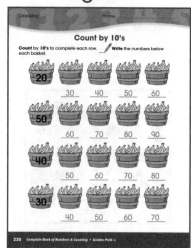

Page 231

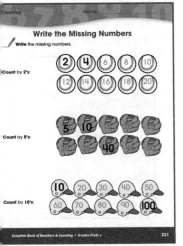

Counting   Name

Write the Missing Numbers

Write the missing numbers.

Count by 2's:
2 4 6 8 10
12 14 16 18 20

Count by 5's:
5 10 15 20 25
30 35 40 45 50

Count by 10's:
10 20 30 40 50
60 70 80 90 100

Complete Book of Numbers & Counting • Grades PreK–1   231

Page 232

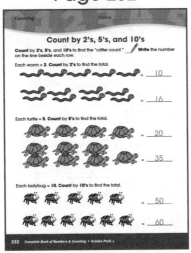

Counting   Name

Count by 2's, 5's, and 10's

Count by 2's, 5's, and 10's to find the "critter count." Write the number on the line beside each row.

Each worm = 2. Count by 2's to find the total.

= 10

= 16

Each turtle = 5. Count by 5's to find the total.

= 20

= 35

Each ladybug = 10. Count by 10's to find the total.

= 50

= 60

232   Complete Book of Numbers & Counting • Grades PreK–1

Page 233

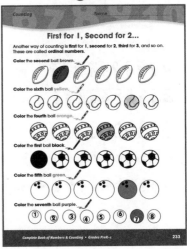

Counting   Name

First for 1, Second for 2...

Another way of counting is **first** for **1**, **second** for **2**, **third** for **3**, and so on. These are called **ordinal numbers**.

Color the **second** ball brown.

Color the **sixth** ball yellow.

Color the **fourth** ball orange.

Color the **first** ball black.

Color the **fifth** ball green.

Color the **seventh** ball purple.

① ② ③ ④ ⑤ ⑥ ⑦ ⑧

Complete Book of Numbers & Counting • Grades PreK–1   233

Page 234

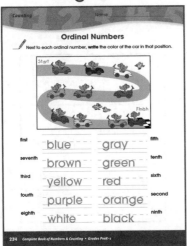

Counting   Name

Ordinal Numbers

Next to each ordinal number, **write** the color of the car in that position.

first	blue	gray	fifth
seventh	brown	green	tenth
third	yellow	red	sixth
fourth	purple	orange	second
eighth	white	black	ninth

234   Complete Book of Numbers & Counting • Grades PreK–1

Page 235

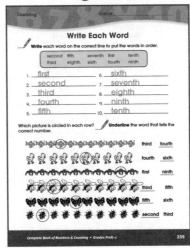

Counting   Name

Write Each Word

Write each word on the correct line to put the words in order.

| second | fifth | seventh | first | tenth |
| third | eighth | sixth | fourth | ninth |

1. first
2. second
3. third
4. fourth
5. fifth
6. sixth
7. seventh
8. eighth
9. ninth
10. tenth

Which picture is circled in each row? **Underline** the word that tells the correct number.

third **fourth**

fourth sixth

first ninth

third fifth

fifth sixth

second third

Complete Book of Numbers & Counting • Grades PreK–1   235

Page 236

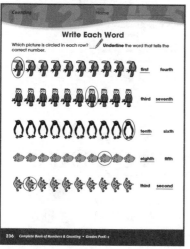

Page 238

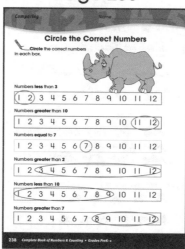

Page 239

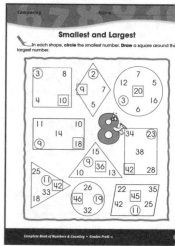

Page 240

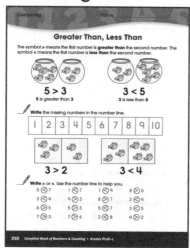

Page 241

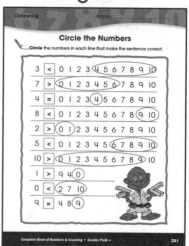

Page 242

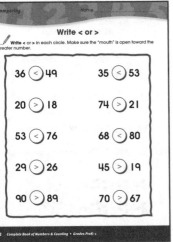

Write < or >

Write < or > in each circle. Make sure the "mouth" is open toward the greater number.

36 < 49   35 < 53

20 > 18   74 > 21

53 < 76   68 < 80

29 > 26   45 > 19

90 > 89   70 > 67

Page 243

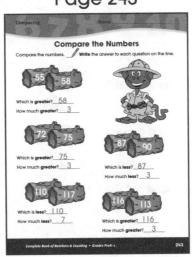

Compare the Numbers

Compare the numbers. Write the answer to each question on the line.

Which is greater? 58
How much greater? 3

Which is greater? 75
How much greater? 3

Which is less? 87
How much less? 3

Which is less? 110
How much less? 7

Which is greater? 116
How much greater? 3

Page 244

Who has the Most?

Who has the most? Circle the correct answer.

1. Traci has **3** s.
   Bob has **4** s.
   Bill has **5** s.
   Who has the **most** s?
   Traci Bob (Bill)

2. Pam has **7** s.
   Joe has **5** s.
   Jane has **6** s.
   Who has the **most** s?
   (Pam) Joe Jane

3. Jennifer has **23** s.
   Sandy has **19** s.
   Jack has **25** s.
   Who has the **most** s?
   Jennifer Sandy (Jack)

4. Ali has **19** s.
   Burt has **18** s.
   Brent has **17** s.
   Who has the **most** s?
   (Ali) Burt Brent

5. The boys have **14** s.
   The girls have **16** s.
   The teachers have **17** s.
   Who has the **most** s?
   boys girls (teachers)

6. Rose has **12** s.
   Betsy has **11** s.
   Leslie has **13** s.
   Who has the **most** s?
   Rose Betsy (Leslie)

Page 245

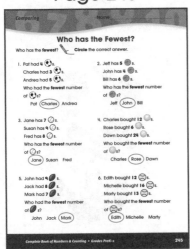

Who has the Fewest?

Who has the fewest? Circle the correct answer.

1. Pat had **4** s.
   Charles had **3** s.
   Andrea had **5** s.
   Who had the **fewest** number of s?
   Pat (Charles) Andrea

2. Jeff has **5** s.
   John has **4** s.
   Bill has **6** s.
   Who has the **fewest** number of s?
   Jeff (John) Bill

3. Jane has **7** s.
   Susan has **9** s.
   Fred has **8** s.
   Who has the **fewest** number of s?
   (Jane) Susan Fred

4. Charles bought **12** s.
   Rose bought **6** s.
   Dawn bought **24** s.
   Who bought the **fewest** number of s?
   Charles (Rose) Dawn

5. John had **9** s.
   Jack had **8** s.
   Mark had **7** s.
   Who had the **fewest** number of s?
   John Jack (Mark)

6. Edith bought **12** s.
   Michelle bought **16** s.
   Marty bought **13** s.
   Who bought the **fewest** number of s?
   (Edith) Michelle Marty

Page 247

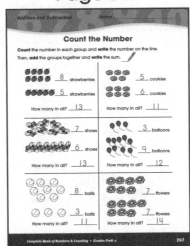

Count the Number

Count the number in each group and write the number on the line.
Then, add the groups together and write the sum.

8 strawberries   5 cookies
5 strawberries   6 cookies
How many in all? 13   How many in all? 11

7 shoes   3 balloons
6 shoes   9 balloons
How many in all? 13   How many in all? 12

8 balls   7 flowers
3 balls   7 flowers
How many in all? 11   How many in all? 14

Page 248

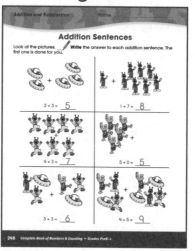

Page 249

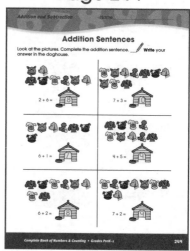

Page 250

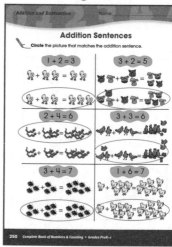

Page 251

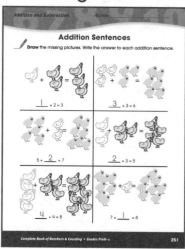

Page 252

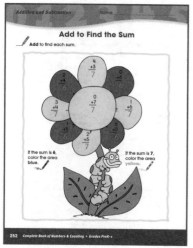

Page 253

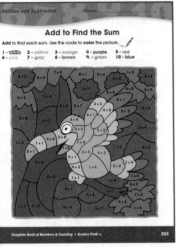

Add to Find the Sum

Add to find each sum. Use the code to **color** the picture.

1 - white   2 - yellow   3 - orange   4 - purple   5 - red
6 - pink   7 - gray   8 - brown   9 - green   10 - blue

Page 254

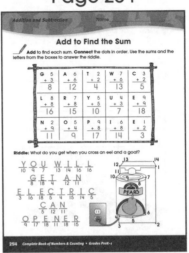

Add to Find the Sum

Add to find each sum. **Connect** the dots in order. Use the sums and the letters from the boxes to answer the riddle.

G 5	A 6	T 2	W 7	C 3
+ 3	+ 6	+ 2	+ 6	+ 2
8	12	4	13	5

L 8	R 7	Y 5	U 4	E 9
+ 8	+ 8	+ 5	+ 9	+ 9
16	15	10	13	18

N 2	O 5	P 9	I 6	E 1
+ 9	+ 4	+ 8	+ 8	+ 2
11	9	17	14	3

Riddle: What do you get when you cross an eel and a goat?

Y O U   W I L L
10 9 13 14 16 15

G E T   A N
8 18 4 11 9

E L E C T R I C
18 16 18 5 4 15 14 13

C A N
5 12 11

O P E N E R
9 17 11 18 3 15

Page 255

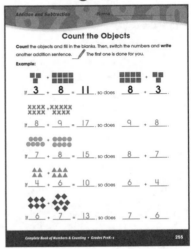

Count the Objects

Count the objects and fill in the blanks. Then, switch the numbers and **write** another addition sentence. The first one is done for you.

Example:

If **3** + **8** = **11**, so does **8** + **3**

If 8 + 9 = 17, so does 9 + 8

If 7 + 8 = 15, so does 8 + 7

If 4 + 6 = 10, so does 6 + 4

If 6 + 7 = 13, so does 7 + 6

Page 256

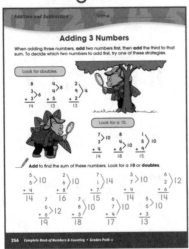

Adding 3 Numbers

When adding three numbers, **add** two numbers first, then **add** the third to that sum. To decide which two numbers to add first, try one of these strategies.

Look for doubles.

8
3 } 6
7
__
14

4
4 } 8
5
__
13

2
2 } 4
9
__
13

Look for a 10.

7
3 } 10
4
__
14

8
6 } 10
6
__
18

1
5 } 10
5
__
15

Add to find the sum of these numbers. Look for a **10** or **doubles**.

5
5 } 10
4
__
14

2
8 } 10
6
__
16

7
7 } 14
1
__
15

3
7 } 10
4
__
14

6
2 } 12
6
__
14

6
6 } 12
7
__
19

3
3 } 10
7
__
18

7
7 } 10
7
__
17

5
5 } 10
3
__
13

Page 257

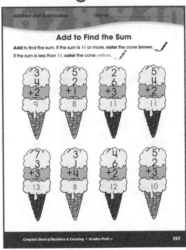

Add to Find the Sum

Add to find the sum. If the sum is 11 or more, **color** the cone brown. If the sum is less than 11, **color** the cone yellow.

3
4
+2
__
9

5
2
+1
__
8

2
6
+3
__
11

5
4
+2
__
11

7
3
+3
__
13

3
1
+4
__
8

4
6
+2
__
12

5
2
+3
__
10

Page 258

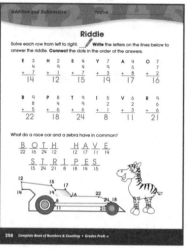

Addition and Subtraction — Name

Riddle

Solve each row from left to right. **Write** the letters on the lines below to answer the riddle. **Connect** the dots in the order of the answers.

E 3 +7 14	H 2 +1 12	S 4 +7 15	Y 7 +3 19	A 4 +8 17	O 7 +2 16

B 9 +5 22	P 8 +4 18	T 9 +6 24	I 5 +2 8	V 6 +3 11	R 9 +6 21

What do a race car and a zebra have in common?

B O T H   H A V E
22 16 24 12   12 17 11 14

S T R I P E S
15 24 21 8 18 14 15

258 *Complete Book of Numbers & Counting • Grades PreK–1*

Page 259

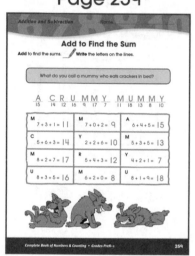

Addition and Subtraction — Name

Add to Find the Sum

Add to find the sums. **Write** the letters on the lines.

What do you call a mummy who eats crackers in bed?

A C R U M M Y   M U M M Y
15 14 12 16 9 17 7   11 18 13 8 10

M 7+3+1= 11	M 7+0+2= 9	A 6+4+5= 15
C 5+6+3= 14	Y 2+2+6= 10	M 5+3+5= 13
M 8+2+7= 17	R 5+4+3= 12	Y 4+2+1= 7
U 8+3+5= 16	M 6+2+0= 8	U 8+1+9= 18

259

Page 260

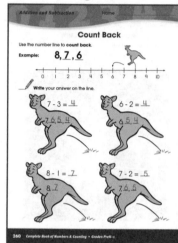

Addition and Subtraction — Name

Count Back

Use the number line to **count back**.

Example: 8, 7, 6

0 1 2 3 4 5 6 7 8 9 10

Write your answer on the line.

7 - 3 = 4
7, 6, 5, 4

6 - 2 = 4
6, 5, 4

8 - 1 = 7
8, 7

7 - 2 = 5
7, 6, 5

260 *Complete Book of Numbers & Counting • Grades PreK–1*

Page 261

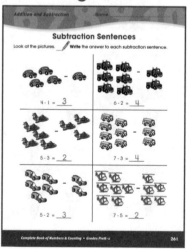

Addition and Subtraction — Name

Subtraction Sentences

Look at the pictures. **Write** the answer to each subtraction sentence.

4 - 1 = 3

6 - 2 = 4

5 - 3 = 2

7 - 3 = 4

5 - 2 = 3

7 - 5 = 2

Complete Book of Numbers & Counting • Grades PreK–1 261

Page 262

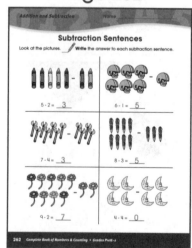

Addition and Subtraction — Name

Subtraction Sentences

Look at the pictures. **Write** the answer to each subtraction sentence.

5 - 2 = 3

6 - 1 = 5

7 - 4 = 3

8 - 3 = 5

9 - 2 = 7

4 - 4 = 0

262 *Complete Book of Numbers & Counting • Grades PreK–1*

Page 263

Page 264

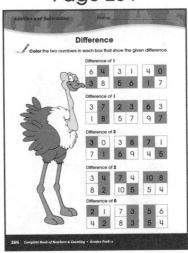

Page 265

Page 266

Page 267

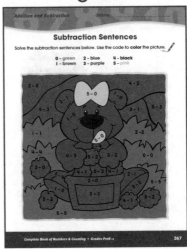

Page 268

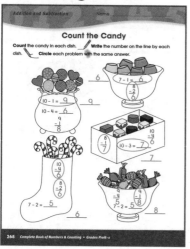

Page 269

Page 270

Page 271

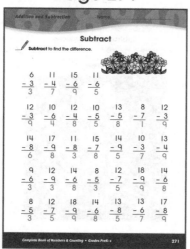

Page 272

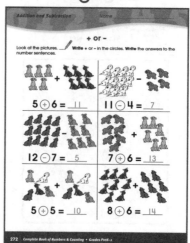

Page 273

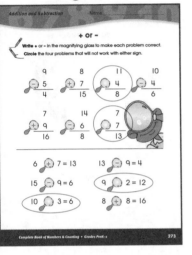

Page 274

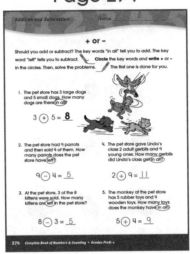

Page 275

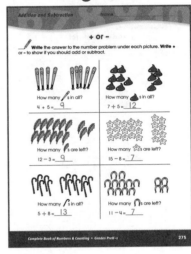

Page 276

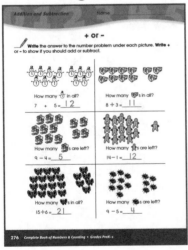

Page 277

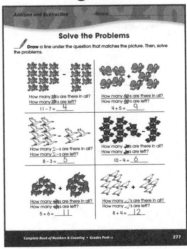

Page 278

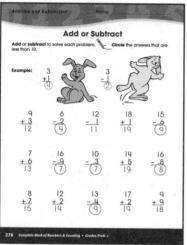

Page 279

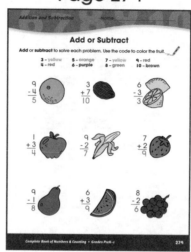

Page 280

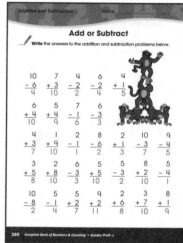

Page 282

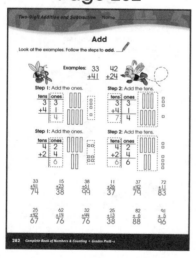

Page 283

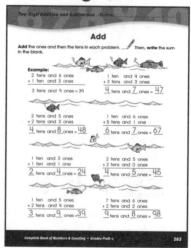

Page 284

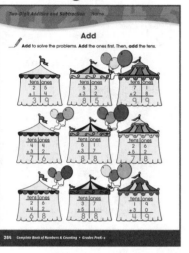

Page 285

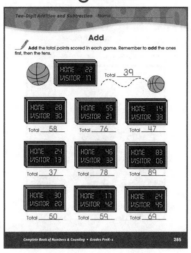

Page 286

Page 287

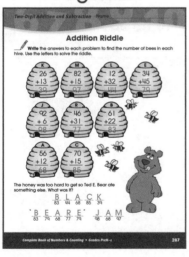

Page 288

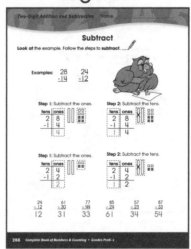

Page 289

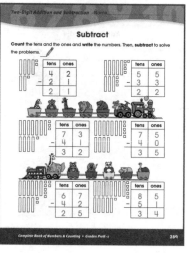

Page 290

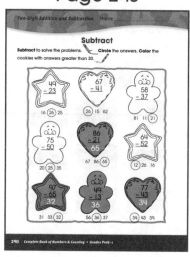

Page 291

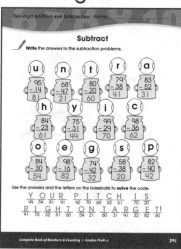

Page 292

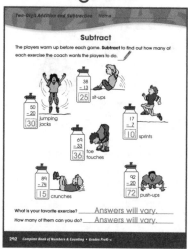

Page 293

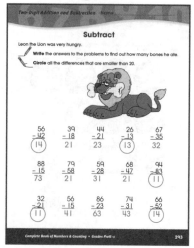

Page 295

Count and Color

Count the apples in each row. Color the boxes to show how many apples have bites taken out of them.

Example:

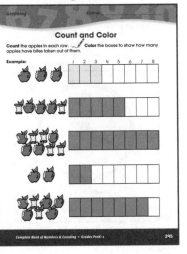

Page 296

Animal Graph

Make a graph of the animals in the jungle. Color one space for each animal.

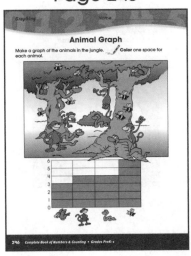

Page 297

Flower Graph

How many of each color flower are there? Color the spaces on the graph below.

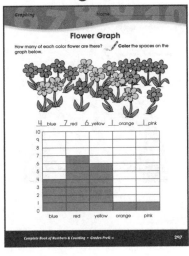

4 blue 7 red 6 yellow 1 orange 1 pink

Page 298

Fruit Graph

Use the information on the bar graph to write the answers to the questions.

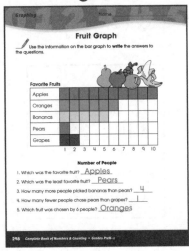

Number of People

1. Which was the favorite fruit? __Apples__
2. Which was the least favorite fruit? __Pears__
3. How many more people picked bananas than pears? __4__
4. How many fewer people chose pears than grapes? __1__
5. Which fruit was chosen by 6 people? __Oranges__

Page 299

Weather Graph

The pictures show the weather for one month. Count the number of sunny, cloudy, and rainy days.

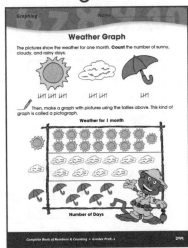

Then, make a graph with pictures using the tallies above. This kind of graph is called a pictograph.

Weather for 1 month

Number of Days

Page 301

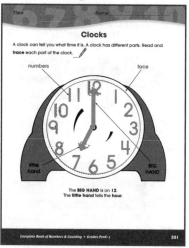

Page 302

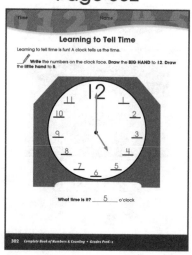

Page 303

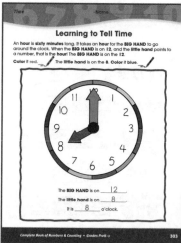

Page 304

Page 305

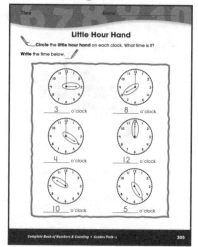

Page 306

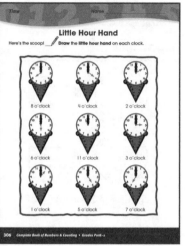

Little Hour Hand

Here's the scoop! Draw the **little hour hand** on each clock.

8 o'clock   4 o'clock   2 o'clock

6 o'clock   11 o'clock   3 o'clock

1 o'clock   5 o'clock   7 o'clock

306   *Complete Book of Numbers & Counting • Grades PreK–1*

Page 307

What Time is it?

What time is it? Write the time on each clock in the blanks below.

7 o'clock   12 o'clock   3 o'clock

6 o'clock   11 o'clock   1 o'clock

8 o'clock   4 o'clock   2 o'clock

9 o'clock   5 o'clock

Complete Book of Numbers & Counting • Grades PreK–1   307

Page 308

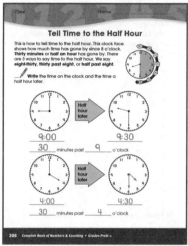

Tell Time to the Half Hour

This is how to tell time to the half hour. This clock face shows how much time has gone by since 8 o'clock. **Thirty minutes** or **half an hour** has gone by. There are 3 ways to say time to the half hour. We say **eight-thirty, thirty past eight,** or **half past eight.**

Write the time on the clock and the time a half hour later.

9:00   Half hour later   9:30

30 minutes past 9 o'clock

4:00   Half hour later   4:30

30 minutes past 4 o'clock

308   *Complete Book of Numbers & Counting • Grades PreK–1*

Page 309

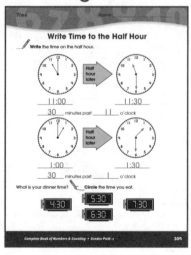

Write Time to the Half Hour

Write the time on the half hour.

11:00   Half hour later   11:30

30 minutes past 11 o'clock

1:00   Half hour later   1:30

30 minutes past 1 o'clock

What is your dinner time? Circle the time you eat.

4:30   5:30   7:30
6:30

Complete Book of Numbers & Counting • Grades PreK–1   309

Page 310

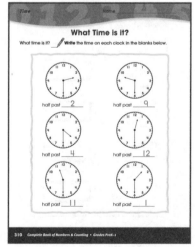

What Time is it?

What time is it? Write the time on each clock in the blanks below.

half past 2   half past 9

half past 4   half past 12

half past 11   half past 1

310   *Complete Book of Numbers & Counting • Grades PreK–1*

Page 311

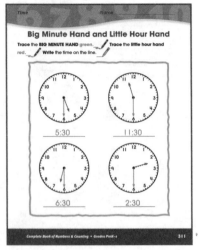

Big Minute Hand and Little Hour Hand

Trace the **BIG MINUTE HAND** green. Trace the **little hour hand** red. **Write** the time on the line.

5:30   11:30

6:30   2:30

Page 312

Who "Nose" These Times?

Write the time under each clock. **Color** the noses.

9:00   9:30   2:00   2:30

5:00   5:30   1:00   1:30

8:00   8:30   11:00   11:30

Page 313

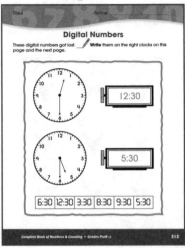

Digital Numbers

These digital numbers got lost. **Write** them on the right clocks on this page and the next page.

12:30

5:30

6:30 | 12:30 | 3:30 | 8:30 | 9:30 | 5:30

Page 314

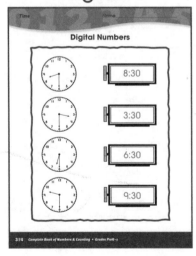

Digital Numbers

8:30

3:30

6:30

9:30

Page 315

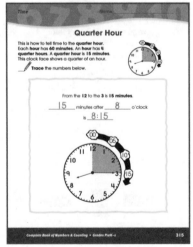

Quarter Hour

This is how to tell time to the **quarter hour**. Each **hour** has **60 minutes**. An **hour** has **4 quarter hours**. A **quarter hour** is **15 minutes**. This clock face shows a quarter of an hour.

Trace the numbers below.

From the **12** to the **3** is **15 minutes**.

15 minutes after 8 o'clock is 8:15

Page 316

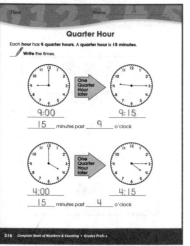

Page 317

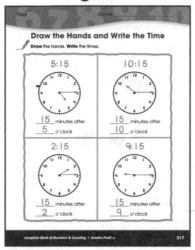

Page 318

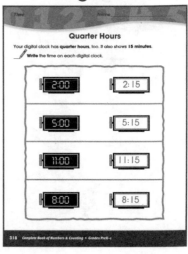

Page 319

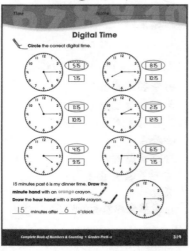

Page 320

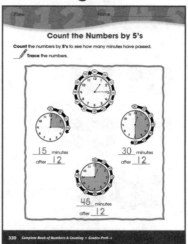

Page 321

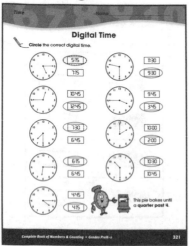

Page 323

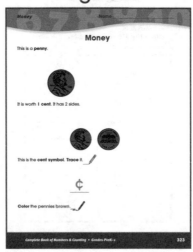

Page 324

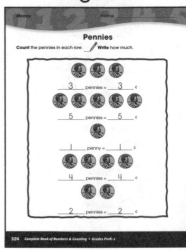

Page 325

Page 326

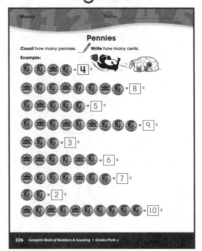

Page 327

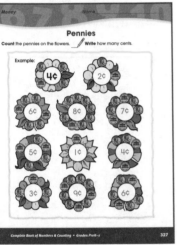

Page 328

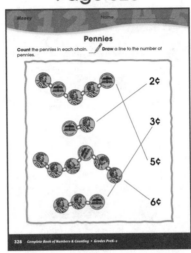

Page 329

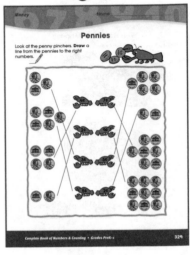

Page 330

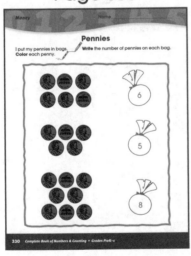

Page 331

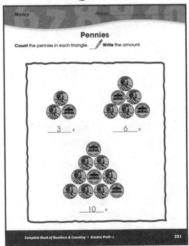

Page 332

Page 333

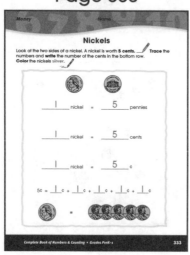

Page 335

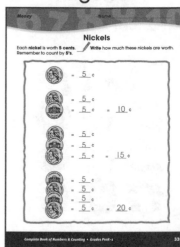

Page 336

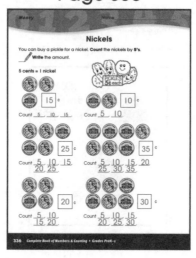

Page 337

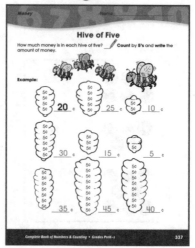

Page 338

Page 339

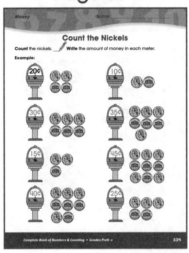

Page 340

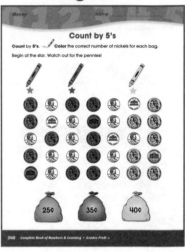

Page 341

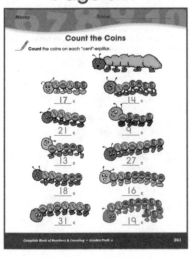

Page 342

Page 343

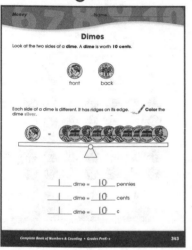

Page 344

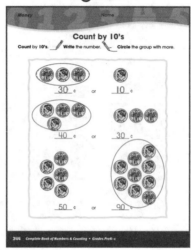

Page 345

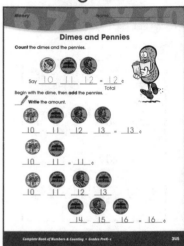

Page 346

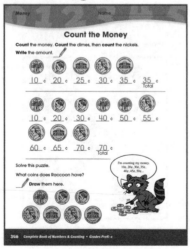

Page 347

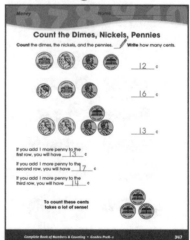

Page 348

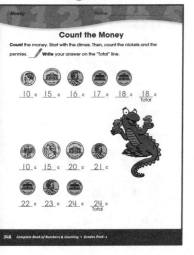

Money   Name _____

Count the Money

Count the money. Start with the dimes. Then, count the nickels and the pennies. **Write** your answer on the "Total" line.

_10_ ¢   _15_ ¢   _16_ ¢   _17_ ¢   _18_ ¢   _18_ ¢ Total

_10_ ¢   _15_ ¢   _20_ ¢   _21_ ¢

_22_ ¢   _23_ ¢   _24_ ¢   _24_ ¢ Total

348   *Complete Book of Numbers & Counting • Grades PreK–1*

Page 349

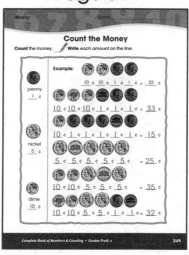

Money   Name _____

Count the Money

Count the money.   **Write** each amount on the line.

penny 1   nickel 5   dime 10

Example:
_10_ ¢ _ 1_ ¢ _ 1_ ¢ = _22_ ¢
_10_ ¢ _10_ ¢ _10_ ¢ _ 1_ ¢ _ 1_ ¢ _ 1_ ¢ = _33_ ¢
_10_ ¢ _ 1_ ¢ _ 1_ ¢ _ 1_ ¢ _ 1_ ¢ _ 1_ ¢ = _15_ ¢
_ 5_ ¢ _ 5_ ¢ _ 5_ ¢ _ 5_ ¢ _ 5_ ¢ = _25_ ¢
_ 5_ ¢ _ 5_ ¢ _ 5_ ¢ _ 5_ ¢ _ 5_ ¢ = _35_ ¢
_10_ ¢ _10_ ¢ _ 5_ ¢ _ 5_ ¢ _ 1_ ¢ _ 1_ ¢ = _32_ ¢

Complete Book of Numbers & Counting • Grades PreK–1   349

Page 350

Money   Name _____

Bake Sale

There is a bake sale at school today. Take some money with you!

19¢   12¢   15¢   9¢   8¢

Decide which one you want. In the space below, draw enough money to pay for it.

Answers will vary.

350   *Complete Book of Numbers & Counting • Grades PreK–1*

Page 351

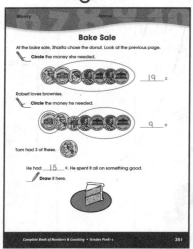

Money   Name _____

Bake Sale

At the bake sale, Sharita chose the donut. Look at the previous page.

Circle the money she needed.

_19_ ¢

Robert loves brownies.

Circle the money he needed.

_9_ ¢

Tom had 3 of these.

He had _15_ ¢. He spent it all on something good.

Draw it here.

Complete Book of Numbers & Counting • Grades PreK–1   351

Page 352

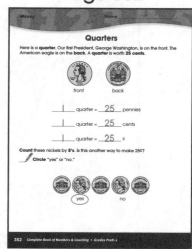

Money   Name _____

Quarters

Here is a **quarter**. Our first President, George Washington, is on the front. The American eagle is on the **back**. A **quarter** is worth **25 cents**.

front   back

_1_ quarter = _25_ pennies

_1_ quarter = _25_ cents

_1_ quarter = _25_ ¢

Count these nickels by **5's**. Is this another way to make 25¢?

Circle "yes" or "no."

(yes)   no

352   *Complete Book of Numbers & Counting • Grades PreK–1*

Page 353

Money   Name

Quarters

These are all ways to make 25¢.

Color each coin.

1 quarter

2 dimes,
1 nickel

5 nickels

25
pennies

Page 354

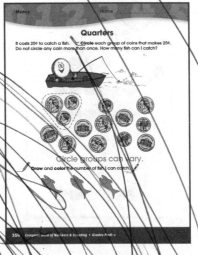

Quarters

It costs 25¢ to catch a fish. **Circle** each group of coins that makes 25¢. Do not circle any coin more than once. How many fish can I catch?

Circle groups can vary.

Draw and **color** the number of fish I can catch.

Page 355

Buying Fruit

Patty bought these pears at the store. She paid **25¢** for each pear.

Color the pears.

25¢ each

Draw the quarters she spent.

How much did she spend? _50_ ¢

Jennifer bought these bananas. She paid **10¢** for each one.

Color the bananas.

10¢ each

Draw the dimes she spent.

How much did she spend? _70_ ¢

Which girl spent less? _Patty_

Page 356

Count the Money

Count the money.   **Write** the amount.

_25_ ¢   _35_ ¢   _45_ ¢   _45_ ¢
                                Total

_25_ ¢   _50_ ¢   _55_ ¢   _55_ ¢
                                Total

Put more than 50¢ in the bank.   **Draw** the coins.

Answer
can vary.

Page 357

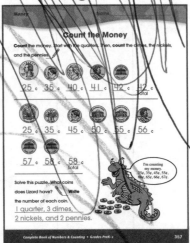

Count the Money

Count the money. Start with the quarters. Then, **count** the dimes, the nickels, and the pennies.

_25_ ¢ _35_ ¢ _40_ ¢ _41_ ¢ _42_ ¢   _42_ ¢
                                          Total

_25_ ¢ _35_ ¢ _45_ ¢ _50_ ¢ _55_ ¢   _56_ ¢

_57_ ¢ _58_ ¢ _58_ ¢
                Total

I'm counting my money. 25¢, 35¢, 45¢, 55¢, 60¢, 65¢, 66¢, 67¢.

Solve this puzzle. What coins does Lizard have?   **Write** the number of each coin.
1 quarter, 3 dimes, 2 nickels, and 2 pennies.

Page 358

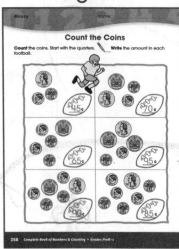

Count the Coins

Count the coins. Start with the quarters.   **Write** the amount in each football.

45¢   70¢

65¢   95¢

90¢   85¢